simple stunning wedding ETIQUETTE

Traditions, Answers, and Advice from One of Today's Top Wedding Planners

KAREN BUSSEN

STEWART, TABORI & CHANG | NEW YORK

contents

introduction

Etiquette. The word itself is intimidating. Say it out loud, *"ehh-tee-keht."* It even sounds proper! It's enough to make us feel as though we should sit up straight and behave ourselves as we read this page.

For those planning a wedding, the subject can become not just intimidating but overwhelming when combined with all the other decisions and factors they must coordinate on the way to creating a beautiful wedding day.

Before the last half of the twentieth century, enormous pressure was put upon hosts (as well as guests) to act appropriately every day, not to mention for such a special occasion as a wedding. Social rules were strict and structured, with unhappy consequences for those who failed to observe proper etiquette. For example, in Victorian England it would have been considered unthinkable for a guest to fail to reply to an invitation to dinner, much less a wedding celebration.

Oh, how times have changed. These days, it is often left to the engaged couple or their families to make phone calls to wayward guests once the reply date for a wedding invitation has passed. "They know I'm coming," has become a common refrain among guilty non-repliers, who don't understand that it is their social *obligation* to reply.

In addition, modern social changes—family structure, couples who'll host their own weddings, even the Internet—have affected how we communicate and the way we celebrate.

Some of that change is good. After all, thanks to computers and the Internet, we can research fabulous wedding products and services, track guest lists, and manage contact information with the click of a mouse. But even though life has never been busier or more wired for efficiency, attention and care should still be given to the art of genuine thoughtfulness, and consideration should not be forgotten. Gracious communication is a beautiful gift we don't want to lose.

Our current social trends and wedding configurations sometimes make us question the former rules of etiquette. Today, for example, brides sometimes have "men of honor" rather than maids, and grooms have "best women." There are same-sex ceremonies and a mix of cultural traditions like never before.

In my experience helping hundreds of couples create their celebrations, I have come across the many questions, concerns, and situations that I'll share with you in this book. We'll talk about everything related to wedding etiquette, from announcing your engagement to starting your new life together, and all the wonderful details in between.

Your wedding should be a unique and personal expression of your love, your families, your traditions, and your hopes and dreams. I am honored to be a part of your celebration and wish you the wedding of your dreams and a lifetime of happiness!

simple stunning
SOLUTIONS

HANDLING ANY ETIQUETTE SITUATION

Chances are good that at some point during your wedding planning you will encounter at least one situation that is delicate, uncomfortable, or downright sticky. While this book covers information, traditions, and ideas for tackling hundreds of wedding-related issues, the specifics of your celebration might be uniquely puzzling or frustrating. Use the following principles (along with more detailed examples of sticky situations and their Simple Stunning solutions in each chapter) to help you sort out the right thing to do in almost any etiquette quandary.

know your priorities

Make a list of the things that are most important to you and your fiancé when it comes to the wedding. Is it that you prefer a small wedding party? Maybe you want a ceremony blending both of your traditions. Or perhaps you don't like sit-down dinners and feel strongly about hosting an informal reception.

Early in the process, make sure to identify and share key objectives, first with each other, then with your parents, your wedding party, and other key people. Remember to do so with kindness and respect. Being open and honest about your needs and wishes will help to avoid misunderstandings, and if conflict arises, you can deal with it right away and move forward with a resolution.

get a firm grip on
what just doesn't matter

Your future mother-in-law has chosen a dress in a color that clashes with your design plan. Your father wants to add several of his important colleagues to your guest list, even though you've never met these people and you want an intimate celebration.

Sometimes little things can seem like a big deal, especially when you factor in emotions, opinions, and stress levels that tend to run high during the wedding planning process. Put things in perspective by reassuring yourself that happy parents are far more desirable than color-coordinated outfits and perfect guest counts. Consider a compromise if it won't affect your top priorities, and always be gracious, even when you must say no.

take care of people with special needs

Whenever you demonstrate that your guests' needs are important to you, you honor the tradition of being a great host. Whether it's providing a vegetarian option on your dinner menu or making sure your grandmother has a quiet seat away from the band, your efforts on behalf of friends and family will be appreciated more than you can ever know.

put on your diplomat hat

Your fiancé's best friend dreams of a singing career and wants to debut his talents at your wedding. An acquaintance from college assumes she'll be in your bridal party. Your two sets of parents disagree on where the wedding should take place. You may be surprised by situations like these, so take the time and effort to be tactful, even if you must refuse an offer or deliver unwanted news. Perhaps you can find a place in your ceremony for your college friend to read a poem, blessing, or passage.

be your guest

Or at least think like one of them. Mailing out a save-the-date card or posting accommodation information on a wedding website for a destination celebration is both thoughtful and practical. Hiring a babysitter to help with young wedding guests will be much appreciated by the parents of said small persons, as well as by every other guest at your party. Think through your timing carefully, and ask yourself, "What might make my guests most comfortable here?" The answer shouldn't have to involve extravagant provisions—just thoughtful consideration.

SAVE *the* DATE...

kindness and common sense— apply as necessary

Let both be your guides whenever you have a choice to make or a problem to solve. Even in difficult or frustrating situations where emotions can come into play, take the high road—every time. And if you have a decision to make, ask yourself, "What really makes sense here?" Sometimes if you just step back and look at the big picture for a moment (or sleep on it overnight), you'll find that the answer is right in front of you.

really listen

This applies to all relationships everywhere, so feel free to apply this Simple Stunning solution at work, home—you name it! Good communication is the root of all good relationships. When a person feels his point of view has been heard, understood, and respected, all things are possible. Listen with an open mind and an open heart, and take time to respond with care and compassion, no matter what the subject.

choose your battles

They really don't need to be battles at all. Sometimes, with emotions on over-load and a lot of little details piling up, the small stuff can induce sleepless nights and create tension between people who love and care for each other. As mentioned above, knowing your priorities will help you identify areas that are really important versus the little things that might be easy to accommo-date. For example, I once sat through seventeen minutes (yes, I timed it) of a meeting with a bride and her in-laws-to-be about which white coffee cup was more perfect to use at a wedding dessert buffet. I generally like to let things like this resolve themselves whenever possible, but at a certain point, the bride and her future mother-in-law turned to me for advice. I simply pointed out that both cups were white and pretty and that what was truly important was to serve a good, hot cup of coffee that guests would enjoy with the delicious cake they had chosen. At that moment, the bride's faced relaxed and she graciously selected the cup her future mother-in-law preferred. Well done!

modern etiquette is not always about rules

It's about doing what's right for your situation. Of course there are still things that are "not done" (like printing, "We prefer cash gifts" on your wedding invitation), but in general, the point is to be considerate, thoughtful, humble, and caring. If there is a choice you can make that suits you and makes your family and guests feel great, too, that is probably the right choice to make, whether or not it falls strictly within the guidelines of what is "proper."

nobody's perfect

As you are putting together the details of your celebration, it can be easy to get caught up in the quest for a flawless wedding. I knew a bride who was devastated when she discovered she'd missed the deadline for submitting her wedding announcement to the *New York Times*. A groom forgot to invite someone who was very important to his parents and was too embarrassed to extend the invitation so close to the wedding date. How could they have overlooked these important elements? The fact is, everyone makes mistakes or forgets something. When you discover your error, take immediate steps to correct it if possible, with a heartfelt apology if appropriate. If the mistake is uncorrectable, chalk it up to experience and move on with the reassuring knowledge that you, too, are only human.

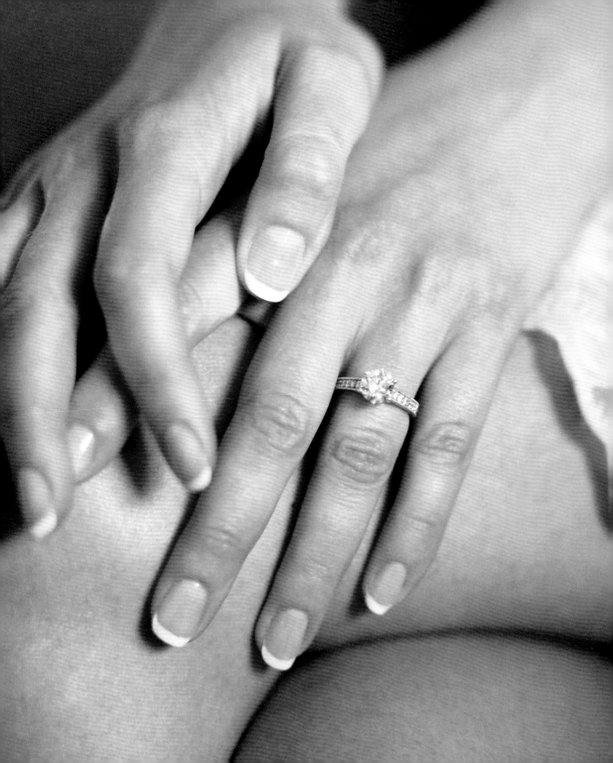

rules of ENGAGEMENT

SHARING THE NEWS WITH FAMILY AND FRIENDS

Joyful news is a wonderful thing to share, and when you've just become engaged, you might feel like running up to the nearest rooftop and proclaiming your love to the whole world. Let tradition (and good old common sense) help you with the order of the telling.

children and parents first

If you or your fiancé have children, they should be the first to know, followed by your parents and grandparents. Next, tell your close friends and extended family. They'll help you spread the news to your wider circle of special people. Finally, share your happiness and excitement with other friends, work supervisors, and colleagues.

what if?

Hopefully the reaction to your engagement will be unanimously positive and everyone will share in the joy and celebration of this happy time. If, however, you encounter a reaction that is negative or unexpected, don't panic.

Children's reactions may be difficult to predict, so share the news in a quiet place, and give them a chance to ask questions if they are curious about details. Hopefully, they will also be thrilled with the announcement, and you can begin making plans to include them in your ceremony and the festivities. If a divorce or other difficult circumstances (such as the death of a parent) are involved, children might be hesitant or hurt to hear that their world will be changing yet again, so give them time and plenty of hugs as they adjust to the news. The decision of whether you and your partner should tell the children together or separately will depend on the situation, but do make sure that as a parent, you allow special alone time with each child to reassure them that your relationship with them remains just as special and important as ever.

If you know you'll have a difficult situation in telling your parents about your engagement, you can choose to tell them together, as a couple, or share the news privately first and then arrange for a meeting together. Sometimes it just takes a little while for the news to set in, so be patient and understanding. Try to imagine how important this moment is to your parents.

Of course, the tradition of a prospective groom asking the bride's parents for her hand is a lovely one, and if the relationship is suited to this kind of rapport, it's a wonderful show of respect and honor.

If you were married before and if circumstances permit, it is thoughtful to tell your ex-spouse personally about the engagement. If children are involved, this is a must. Be humble and considerate, and resist any temptation to over-emphasize your incredible happiness.

extra! extra!

If you'd like to announce your engagement, consider publishing an announcement in your local newspaper. Call the editorial offices or check the paper's website for guidelines, as some papers print wedding announcements (after

Engagement

DO

- Early on in the process, check with your local and state authorities to determine what the criteria are for you to be married. It's easy to do this research on your local government office website (search "marriage" or "marriage bureau"). You'll want to know what the requirements are for things like your marriage license, health tests (not required everywhere), residency, age, and other issues.

- Meet the parents. Hopefully, you've already met each other's parents by the time you get engaged, but if not, you should make plans to do so. Next, make sure all the parents have a chance meet each other if possible. It doesn't matter who hosts (traditionally it was the groom's family) or where the meeting takes place.

- Set a date that works for you. You're not bound by any specific time frame, although most engagements last somewhere between six months and a year and a half on average. If you're planning a destination wedding, you'll want to allow a bit more time for guests to arrange schedules and travel plans. And of course if another family member or very close friend has a conflict, take that into consideration when choosing your date.

DON'T

- Don't print a special card to announce your engagement. Although a wedding announcement card may be mailed after the ceremony (for those who didn't attend the celebration), the news of your engagement should be shared personally by phone, letter, or email as described above. In a situation where one partner is in the process of a divorce, never announce your engagement until the divorce is official and final.

- Don't forget to take time to enjoy each other and this precious time in your lives. Spend a few days or weeks just soaking up the excitement of being engaged and in love before you jump into the planning process.

the ceremony) but not engagement notices. Many papers that do publish announcements offer simple online forms to complete. Applicants provide key family names (bride, groom, parents, grandparents) and information about the couple (education, career details, and so on). From this information, staff writers draft the copy for the announcement. Sometimes there is a small fee involved, and some papers allow you to send in or upload an engagement photo with your submission.

engagement party basics

There are so many wonderful celebrations that dot the social calendars of those about to be married, and the engagement party is usually the first. Anyone can host an engagement get-together, although often it is one set of parents (or even both sets together or separately) who do the honors. Other possible hosts for the engagement party include siblings, close friends or relatives, or a combination. Guests are not required to bring gifts, although it's not a bad idea to get your wedding registry in order in the event that guests might ask the host for those details (see the Please and Thank You chapter [page 73] for more information on registry and gifts).

An engagement celebration is often an informal party, held at home, but these days it could take place in a modern loft or in a private room of a restaurant. It might be a cocktail party, a Sunday brunch, an afternoon barbecue, or a family-style dinner. You could decorate with photos of the two of you, and you might even have a formal portrait taken as a memory of this special time.

The host of the engagement party is responsible for sending out invitations, providing decorations and refreshments, and giving a welcome speech or toast at the party. They might need your help with a list of names and addresses of folks you'd like to attend the party, but before submitting a giant list, make sure to find out how many guests the host is planning for because space and cost may be a factor.

engagement rings and wedding bands

In the past, choosing an engagement ring was the prospective groom's responsibility. But for modern couples, this element is often a wonderful, shared experience, with the majority of brides involved in selecting their engagement rings.

There are many styles of rings and many options to consider—gold, silver, and platinum; marquis and emerald cuts; stone size and quality. The thing to remember is that while it is a beautiful tradition, an engagement ring is not necessary for a couple to become engaged.

STICKY SITUATION	SIMPLE STUNNING SOLUTION
My fiancé's mother wants me to wear his grand-mother's engagement ring, but it's not my style.	You are not obligated to wear a ring you don't like. Discuss the situation with your fiancé first, and tell his mother that you are honored and delighted by the offer, but you're making other plans for your ring.
A lot of our family and friends live far away. Can we email our good news?	For close relatives, a phone call is better. Email is fine for distant relatives and friends, but it's better to address each email individually rather than sending a mass e-missive to the whole group.
We just got engaged and my groom has already brought up the topic of a pre-nuptial agreement.	This is something you have to discuss in detail together. While in the past, pre-nups, as they're often called, were designed to protect a partner with signif-icant financial assets, more and more couples are opting to formalize arrangements for if and when the marriage doesn't work. This is probably the stickiest of sticky situations. Really listen, communicate honestly, and if necessary, seek professional advice to determine if a pre-nuptial document is right for you.
We're calling off the wedding. What do we do?	Inform your inner circle first. Brides should return the engagement ring. Any gifts that have been received should also be returned with a simple note explaining that the engagement has been called off. On the practical side, inform all of your vendors in writing, and be aware that you may lose deposits or payments. Calling off a wedding takes courage. Take the high road and show respect for each other in this difficult time. While neither scenario is easy, it is better to call off an engagement than to end a marriage.

When selecting rings, visit stores and research the types and styles available so you can determine what works best for you. Think about your lifestyle and your work when considering what type of ring you'll want to wear every day. Bridal magazines often feature articles on all the particulars of carat, cut, clarity, and so forth, and you can also find a lot of helpful information on the Internet. The Resource Guide (page 120) has great ring-related books and websites.

WHAT ABOUT WEDDING BANDS? Most couples wear wedding bands that coordinate with each other in some way, but you can choose what you prefer. The exchange of wedding rings is a part of most wedding ceremonies, and the circle is thought to symbolize never-ending love and unity. When it comes to styles of wedding bands, again, there are many options, from handmade pieces created by local artisans to classic styles available in fine jewelry stores. If you will wear wedding bands, an engraving of your initials or a sweet message on the inside of the ring is a lovely touch, so make sure to ask if your rings can be engraved.

RINGS AT THE CEREMONY On the wedding day, you may choose to wear your engagement ring by moving it to your right hand, or you could opt to wear just your wedding band. After the wedding, women often wear the engagement ring and wedding band together, or they might just wear the wedding band and save the engagement ring for special occasions, depending upon their profession or the size of the ring. You should do what's best for your lifestyle and comfort.

money MATTERS

During the planning of a wedding, with all its emotions, details, excitement, and stress, the subject of money can be a delicate and sensitive one. Whether it's the bride's parents, the groom's family, the couple themselves, or some combination of the three who are providing the financing for the celebration, the topic involves so much more than just how much to spend on flowers or music.

Before you begin the process of planning the details of your ceremony and reception, have an open discussion with your fiancé to determine your priorities for the wedding. Chances are you'll already have some idea of who will pay for your celebration, and creating a list of what's most important to you will allow you to guide both your spending and your interactions related to wedding funds. If you would like help with determining your priorities and budgeting for all your wedding expenses, take a look at the Resource Guide (page 120).

Once you've discussed your priorities, determine with your families, if appropriate, who will be contributing, and what the overall budget for the celebration will be. In the United States, the average cost of a wedding is more than twenty thousand dollars, but a beautiful wedding is not really about dollars and cents. My feeling is that the most fabulous weddings are the ones that are brimming with happiness, individuality, and a truly festive spirit, regardless of the number of flowers on the tables or the size of the band.

who pays for what?

Of course, tradition held specific roles and responsibilities for each of the parties in a wedding. These days, many brides and grooms are a bit older and more financially independent, or often both sets of parents will want to contribute to the wedding budget. Today's couples create their budget arrangements based upon their own unique needs and wishes, but below you will find a brief accounting of traditional responsibilities for wedding costs.

here comes the bride (with checkbook)

The bride's family typically paid for the bride's gown and accessories; the groom's wedding ring; invitations and all printed materials; accommodations and transportation for the bride and her attendants (to and from the ceremony and reception); all floral arrangements (except the bride's flowers), decor, and music for the ceremony and reception; the wedding reception itself (food, photography, and so forth); and the bride's gifts to both her groom and her attendants. A luncheon or party for the bride's attendants would also be her family's responsibility.

proper grooming

The groom's family was responsible for paying for the groom's attire (plus accessories for his attendants such as special ties, cummerbunds, or vests); fees for the marriage license and officiant; and the rehearsal dinner. In addition, the groom's family was expected to provide accommodations and transportation for the groom and his attendants (to and from the ceremony and reception); the groom's gifts for his bride and his attendants; and, of course, the honeymoon. If the groom were to host a luncheon or dinner for his attendants, his family would be responsible for those expenses as well.

perfect attendants

Attendants of both the bride and groom were traditionally responsible for any necessary travel expenses, although their accommodations would be paid for by the family of the bride or groom. Attendants have always paid for their attire and accessories, although many brides these days give their attendants necklaces or earrings to wear at the celebration. If there were an attendant for whom it would be a financial hardship to bear the cost of travel or attire, the couple might decide to assist with those expenses at their own discretion. It is never bad form to be kind, considerate, or helpful!

Attendants often pool funds for gifts to the bride and groom, and in addition, they typically pay for the bachelor and bachelorette parties and sometimes foot the bill for the wedding shower.

a blooming nice tradition

It used to be the sweet custom in some places that the groom's family would pay for the bride's bouquet as well as the groom's attendants' lapel flowers, but typically today there is just one florist for the whole event who provides all the personal flowers for the ceremony (bouquets, lapel flowers, baskets for the flower girls, and corsages or nosegays for mothers and grandmothers). As with all the other wedding expenses today, it's perfectly acceptable for each couple to determine what works best for them.

It is, however, a wonderful idea to honor the lovely tradition that the groom's lapel flower, or boutonniere, is a blossom "plucked" from the bride's bouquet. How romantic!

staying on track

In my experience, wedding budgets can be compared to gardens in the summertime. They need constant attention or they might grow out of control, or worse—dry up unexpectedly! I suggest creating a budget spreadsheet in

STICKY SITUATION	SIMPLE STUNNING SOLUTION
A lot of our wedding vendors are asking for final payment before the wedding date. Is this normal?	Yes. Many wedding professionals require advance payment (or final payment on the wedding day itself). Read all contracts carefully and ask for clarification on any unclear points related to payment and terms, and get receipts and contract updates throughout the process.
We don't have enough cash to pay for the whole wedding and want to get new credit cards to help finance the cost.	Beware of over-spending on your wedding, especially where credit cards are involved. Of course, you can gain airline miles or rewards points for some purchases, which can be great, but you can also incur large finance charges if you don't pay off balances right away. If this is your first time budgeting for big purchases together, use it as a chance to set goals and limits and stay within them. You'll be so much happier when you get back from the honeymoon and you've still got money in the bank.
Our parents are offering to pay for the wedding only if we have the celebration they envision, with their friends, at a location of their choosing.	It's true that sometimes money equals power. And proud parents often want to help craft what they feel will be the best possible situation. Really listen to what they're proposing. Perhaps part of their plan is acceptable. Ask if there is any room to negotiate on guest counts, or show them a location you like and see if you can win them over. If not, you may decide to compromise, or to host and pay for the wedding yourself and let them contribute only partially.

Excel or your favorite software program and using it to track estimated costs, deposits, and actual expenses along the way.

The fact is that the final price tag for your wedding will be determined by the choices you make along the way. Flowers, music, food, wine—every aspect of a wedding offers the opportunity to customize and upgrade, and even small upgrades over the course of many decisions can result in unwanted overages. Knowing your priorities is crucial. Then, if you monitor your costs as you go, you can easily see where you're spending more than you thought you would, or where you can tweak to save a bit here and there.

how to create a wedding budget

There are so many variables in every wedding celebration that affect the final budget. Do you have a large or small guest list? What's the size of your bridal party? Will you have live music or a DJ? Are you crazy about flowers?

Knowing your priorities will help you set your budget guidelines. Once you've determined how much money you have to spend on the celebration as a whole, you can begin to allot finances and make adjustments as you go.

Hiring a wedding coordinator can actually be good for your budget, as they can sometimes negotiate on your behalf and share their expertise regarding overall budgets and specific costs for things like venue rental, tablecloths, and bands. Once they know what's important to you, a good planner can likely give you an educated estimate for what the whole shebang might set you back.

If you don't wish to have a wedding coordinator, you'll need to spend time doing some research as to what things cost in your area. Make phone calls or send emails to a few wedding pros and start gathering information before you make any financial commitments.

I suggest creating a detailed budget estimate for your wedding, filling in specifics as you look at proposals and options. If you make one expensive choice, you can use your detailed budget to look at other areas where you might be able to cut back.

working with vendors

This may sound obvious, but get everything in writing, including proposals, contracts, and agreements (and any updates or revisions). This will help keep your relationship with vendors on track and will help you manage your budget as you evaluate estimated costs against actual costs.

wedding insurance

You should make sure that every vendor you hire for your wedding is fully covered with regard to liability and worker's comp. Ask for copies of each and every vendor's insurance certificate, and request to have yourself named as an additional insured on the certificate.

You can also purchase insurance for your own coverage. More and more couples are choosing to insure their wedding celebrations. While this is not an etiquette issue, it sure can be valuable in the case of cancellation or postponement, or in the event of an accident. There are companies that now specialize in event insurance. Speak to your insurance broker about the type of coverage that's right for you. Event day coverage can often be added to your homeowner's policy for liability, and cancellation or postponement insurance will safeguard your deposits and payments if a service provider should fail to show up or if you should decide to put off the celebration.

tipping at your wedding

Tipping is one of those wedding subjects that confounds everyone—sometimes even me! Whom to tip and how much varies greatly according to the situation. Typically, the first thing you want to look at when deciding whom to tip is the type of service that's being provided and whether a gratuity or service charge is already included.

For example, some caterers include a staff gratuity or service charge on their invoices, which makes it easy for brides and grooms (provided, of course, you are happy with the service). Of course you can tip or not tip anyone you please. A gratuity is an extra. But certain folks depend on gratuities as a part of their earnings. Here are some guidelines for vendors to tip and not to tip, but if in your own wedding preparations you are ever unsure, it is not inappropriate (in fact, it's thoughtful) to ask your wedding planner or individual vendors for gratuity guidelines.

TIP A note of heartfelt thanks is one of the best gifts you can give any of your wedding service providers. Just as with any thank-you note, try to recount a few specific things that made the day really special, and mention the names of any individuals who were particularly helpful. If you've felt a special bond with one or more of your wedding providers, a thoughtful gift might be more appropriate than a cash gratuity.

TIP THEM

If a gratuity has not been provided for the following people in your contract, consider rewarding them with a tip.

- **Banquet managers, captains, bartenders, and wait staff** You can calculate this at anywhere between twelve and twenty percent of your food and beverage bill, or ask your planner or banquet director what would be appropriate. Again, make sure this is not already included in your fees. And do not tip on sales tax.
- **Band, ceremony musicians, and DJ** This also varies, as some bands include gratuity in their pricing. If you love your band or ceremony musicians, you can tip each musician individually or prepare one larger amount and give it to the bandleader for distribution. You are not obligated to tip

your band, but again, if they've made your party amazing, you might want to acknowledge that.

- **Drivers** Bus, limousine, and car drivers generally derive part of their income from tips. Check your agreements to see whether gratuity has been included, as it often is. If so, nothing additional is necessary. If not, look at each job individually and tip accordingly.
- **Bathroom and coat check attendants** These hardworking folks are often highly dependent upon tips for their income. Make arrangements for

There are several ways to distribute gratuities. Generally, they are handed out at the end of the celebration, in envelopes or gift cards with the name of the service provider. If gratuity is not included in your catering bill, you do not have to prepare individual tips for each of the wait staff. Rather, set one larger gratuity amount aside and give it to your banquet or catering manager to distribute. Separate catering gratuities are appropriate for key players such as the captains at your event (I suggest asking for their names in advance). If you don't want to distribute envelopes on your wedding night, you can ask your best man or your wedding planner to take care of them for you.

Cash or checks? Most people prefer cash gratuities, but it is your prerogative to tip with a check if you prefer to keep a record.

If you'd prefer to wait till after the celebration to tip key staff members, this is fine, but remember that it may be more difficult for the catering company to distribute gratuities to the appropriate wait staff weeks later, as many of these workers are freelancers. Of course if you do tip after the fact, do not send cash in the mail!

their gratuities in advance so that your guests will not feel obligated to tip at the party. If you do tip in advance on behalf of your guests, make sure the venue staff has been informed and that any tip jars or signs that say, "tips appreciated" are removed. In fact, make sure those tacky signs and jars are removed even if you haven't arranged an advance gratuity. Some service providers will post a sign at your request near coat check or valet parking spots to indicate that gratuities have been taken care of by the host.

- **Venue staff** If you're renting a space that requires an on-site venue manager, porters, or other staff to receive rentals or coordinate your wedding setup, consider rewarding them for their help. Ask your representative at the venue to let you know what would be appropriate.

- **Hair and makeup professionals** A small gratuity is always appropriate for these beauty artists, whether you visit the salon or have them come to you on the big day.

NO NEED TO TIP THEM

- **Photographers, videographers, bakers, and florists** These pros charge flat fees for their goods and services and don't generally expect tips. Of course you can tip them if you like, and certainly they'll appreciate it, but a heartfelt note of thanks and possibly a small gift is just fine.

- **Wedding coordinator** This really depends upon your arrangement. No gratuity is expected, but gifts or tips are appropriate if you feel your planner has gone above and beyond to make your day special.

- **Officiants** Often, an officiant may charge a fee or request a donation for performing your wedding ceremony. Donations (even beyond what they've requested) are always appropriate, but a small gift and note of thanks is a better way to show your appreciation for the important part your officiant plays in your wedding.

guest list and
BRIDAL PARTY 101

creating your guest list

Before you can choose your location, order invitations, or hire a caterer, you need to get a general handle on who is coming to the celebration. Do you have a small wedding in mind or something that includes your extended family and friends?

Brides and grooms often experience frustration when trying to put together their perfect list. Just gathering correct and current addresses is a big project, especially if parents or others will be contributing names to the list. Discuss the details of how you'll structure your guest list so that it's easy to control from the very beginning.

Choose a format for collecting your information. You can use a software program and import your contact names and addresses into a list, or you can write the names and numbers on paper for a start. Whatever your preference, make sure that everyone follows the same format. This will make life much easier when you're ready to integrate multiple lists.

Organize your list by group so you can see how your numbers stack up. Your first group would be immediate family and closest friends. Once you have that number, you can see how much room you have for other guests, based on your preferences and your budget. Then you can create groups of other guests (extended family, work colleagues, school friends, and so forth) and use those groups as criteria for deciding whom to include or exclude. Grouping your guest list will help you keep an overall perspective on whom to invite, and it will help you identify issues you'll want to consider. For example, if you invite second cousin Sue, you might need to invite four other sets of second cousins, which could push your guest list over the top.

Guest List
DOS & DON'TS

DO

- Appoint a "master of the list." Once you put your list together, designate one person in charge of changes and updates rather than letting everyone make changes to the same document. This will keep you organized and minimize mistakes.

- Check your list for spelling and address errors. It's better to call and verify now than to take a guess and get the invitation back in the mail later.

DON'T

- Don't invite more people than you can afford. A smaller party is better if it is within your budget.

- Don't invite people you hope won't come. An invitation to your wedding should be extended with sincerity and hospitality. Also, don't invite more guests than your venue can accommodate. What will you do if they all decide your wedding is not to be missed?

- Don't forget to invite live-in partners or spouses of invited guests. No exceptions. You are not required, however, to allow single people to bring a guest, or to invite children to your wedding, nor should you be pressured into doing so. Your invitations will convey exactly who is invited, as we'll discuss in the Invitation Only chapter (page 51).

When compiling your list, remember that consistency is gracious. If you define the parameters of your list by group, it will be much easier for you when you are making decisions about whom to invite. In other words, if you decide to have an adults-only reception, it's much easier to explain that choice than if you choose to invite the kids of certain guests but not those of others.

choosing your bridal party

Traditionally, brides selected a maid or matron of honor and bridesmaids. Grooms gathered a symmetrical collection of a best man and groomsmen. Flower girls or ring bearers were sometimes added to the mix, but generally speaking there was a solid model to follow and not much deviation from it. Roles were very specific for each member of the wedding party, and social convention ruled even who sat next to whom at the reception.

These days, there is a lot less emphasis on matching numbers (or even gender for that matter!). The face of the bridal party is changing. When you are assembling your attendants, you don't need to worry about filling in the proper blanks to fit a certain format. You must simply ask yourself which fine people you'll want to support you throughout your engagement and your wedding celebration. You can combine men and women as attendants, and there's no need for matching numbers on both sides.

Some couples opt to have just a small group of attendants or no bridal party at all. This is particularly true for those who are remarrying, but smaller bridal parties are a growing trend. Some religious institutions have a limit on the number of bridal attendants who can stand with the couple during the ceremony, so if you're considering a large wedding party, make sure to check with your officiant before making your final plans.

However you prefer to configure your bridal party, there are tasks and duties related to the wedding that will need to be completed as a part of the planning or managed on the day of the celebration itself. Asking someone to be in your bridal party is an honor, but it also involves responsibilities, both financial and in terms of time and commitment, so consider how those responsibilities will affect your attendants when thinking about whom to ask.

Here's a description of some of the responsibilities of bridal party members, and some things to consider when selecting yours.

THE BRIDE AND GROOM

As everyone knows, the bride has always been the star of the show, the focal point of the wedding day. In the old days, along with her mother, she would plan all aspects of the celebration, choosing flowers, cake, menu, invitations, and other details. This was her first opportunity to shine as a hostess and be celebrated as a new wife. And there is still nothing like that moment when the bride—glowing, happy, and beautiful—makes her entrance at the ceremony.

The groom, on the other hand, was chiefly responsible for showing up on time (with the help of his best man), smartly dressed and ready to wed.

But for today's brides and grooms, the process of planning and designing their celebration has become much more of a co-production, and couples are more interested in creating a ceremony and reception that reflect a combination of both their styles and their traditions and cultural backgrounds. Because many brides and grooms both work full time and often are contributing to the cost of the wedding (or paying for it entirely), they regularly share the duties of making phone calls and inquiries, running errands, and managing tasks like writing thank-you notes for wedding gifts.

The bride is typically still a bit more involved in the day-to-day planning, but grooms often attend meetings and offer their input about everything from song playlists to reception design and even the wording of the invitations.

As you talk with your fiancé about the wedding, come to an understanding about what works best for you as a couple. There is really no set rule about who does what anymore, so it's a good idea at the beginning of your engagement to talk about how the process should work for you. Deciding who will be responsible for what and how you'll handle the decision-making process throughout your wedding planning will help to keep things sailing along smoothly.

Planning the ceremony together. Designing your marriage ceremony is one of the most special aspects of planning your wedding, as it will be the single most important moment of the day when you begin your new lives together as partners. Speak with your officiant about the process, and spend time talking with each other about this wonderful aspect of your wedding. Whether you'll have a religious or civil ceremony, working together to create your ceremony gives you a wonderful chance to enjoy the beauty, excitement, and anticipation of the day when you'll start your journey together. Research readings and poems, listen to music together, and infuse your ceremony with meaningful details that celebrate your unique love story. See more about this subject in the Ceremony chapter (page 85).

Decisions, decisions. There are so many options, decisions, and details involved in planning a wedding. Food, flowers, music, photography—it can be overwhelming. It's helpful to determine up front who will be involved in the various aspects of the planning process. Here is a list of some of the tasks you might need to manage along the way. Decide what you'll tackle together or who will be responsible for coordinating each area.

- Choosing a venue for your ceremony and reception
- Interviewing wedding planners
- Selecting music for all aspects of the celebration
- Hiring a photographer and videographer
- Designing printed items like save-the-date cards, invitations, and programs

- Creating the look of your celebration with flowers, lighting, and other decor
- Finalizing your menu, wedding cake, wines, and cocktails
- Booking accommodations and reserving transportation
- Choosing attire for yourselves and the wedding party
- Planning your seating for the reception
- Organizing toasts and moments (first dance, cake cutting, and so on)
- Managing budgets, contracts, payments, and gratuities
- Wrapping welcome bags or guest favors

MAID OR MATRON OF HONOR

This honor attendant might be a relative or a very close friend. She attends wedding-related events leading up to the big day and often helps organize a bridal shower, bachelorette festivities, and the bridesmaids' luncheon, along with the bridesmaids' gift to the bride. She'll help with details like choosing bridesmaids' dresses, and she makes sure the bridesmaids are on time, dressed, and ready for the ceremony.

During the ceremony, she'll help the bride with her dress, hold the bride's flowers and the groom's ring, and, like the best man, she'll witness the signing of the marriage certificate. These days, the maid of honor often makes a toast at the wedding reception, and she helps gather the bride's things at the end of the reception, making sure any precious items from the ceremony and reception (prayer books, family photos, ketubah, veil, wedding cake topper, and so forth) are safely packed and transported to the couple's home. Although bouquet and garter tosses are becoming less popular, the maid of honor would participate if these activities are a part of the celebration.

BEST MAN

The best man is a person who is very close to the groom, either a sibling, relative, or important friend. He supports the groom as he prepares in the months leading up to the wedding, attending all wedding-related events. He makes arrangements and organizes details for the bachelor party. He is generally responsible for making a toast at the wedding reception, and often will also speak at the rehearsal dinner.

The best man assures that the groom has his wedding outfit in order, and that he and the other groomsmen are dressed and ready in time on the big day. He traditionally stands up at the ceremony in support of the groom; holds the bride's wedding band; witnesses the signing of the marriage certificate; and often helps with tasks like making sure the officiant's fees have been paid, distributing gratuities, and insuring that gifts received are secure at the couple's home if they'll be leaving right away for the honeymoon. If applicable, he helps coordinate the groomsmen's gift to the couple and wraps up any loose details on behalf of the groom while the couple is on the honeymoon.

BRIDE'S ATTENDANTS

The bride may choose a group of ladies or a combination of men and women to serve as her attendants. They participate in all or most of the pre-wedding parties, plus the ceremony rehearsal and rehearsal dinner. They traditionally stand up in support of the bride and are a part of the receiving line if there is one. They take part in reception activities such as the bouquet toss, if applicable. Bride's attendants sometimes give a toast at the rehearsal dinner or wedding reception, and they may choose to give a group gift or individual gifts to the couple.

GROOM'S ATTENDANTS

The groom may choose male and female attendants, who will be a part of all the festivities leading up to the wedding. Like the bride's attendants, they'll attend wedding-related events, including the bachelor party, ceremony rehearsal, and rehearsal dinner, and they'll typically stand up in support of the groom at the ceremony itself, although sometimes they are seated. If the wedding is small, the groom's attendants might serve as ushers, welcoming (and sometimes seating) guests, and possibly passing out programs or yarmulkes. Groom's attendants are ambassadors of hospitality for the whole celebration, offering help and assistance to guests who might need directions or who have special needs. Sometimes they'll give a toast at the wedding reception, and they'll be responsible for making sure any rented formal wear is returned after the wedding.

USHERS

For larger weddings, it can be nice to appoint a few special people to act as ushers. These ladies and gentlemen are separate from the wedding party, and they act as greeters at the ceremony, welcoming guests and passing out programs, answering questions, and sometimes seating guests. Although they don't walk in the processional or stand up during the ceremony, they might wear a special flower to identify them as ushers, or they can simply position themselves near the entrance. After the ceremony, they are responsible for retrieving extra programs and other items in their charge, making sure they are returned to the bride and groom at the end of the celebration.

FLOWER GIRLS AND JUNIOR BRIDESMAIDS

Flower girls are traditionally younger (usually under the age of eight), and there may be just one flower girl or a group of young ladies who walk down the aisle right before the bride's entrance. They might scatter petals or simply carry pretty posies, and they can be accompanied down the aisle by a ring bearer. Flower girls often take a seat once they've walked down the aisle, joining the recessional walk up the aisle at the end of the ceremony.

A junior bridesmaid is typically anywhere between eight and thirteen years old and has basically the same role as any bridesmaid, with the exception that it is usually her parents who pay for her attire and her gift to the couple.

RING BEARER

Traditionally, this was a young boy, carrying a pillow to which the wedding bands had been tied. Recently, I have seen a number of ring bearers who are young ladies, and either is just fine. He walks in the wedding processional (usually just after the maid of honor), and is often seated for the ceremony, especially if very young. Often the "rings" are just faux rings, as it can be a bit too much responsibility for a very young person to handle important and expensive jewelry.

INVOLVING YOUR OWN CHILDREN

Of course if you have children, you might wish to involve them in the ceremony. They can certainly participate in the classic roles of bridesmaids and groomsmen (or even maid of honor and best man). If you'd like to include a very small child, or if you are blending families (with children from previous relationships on both sides), speak with your officiant about the idea of a family blessing during the service, where the whole family can gather for a special moment in a celebration of unity. For small children, make sure you hire a helper to be on hand throughout the wedding, so the little ones can play or rest quietly if the need arises.

If you'll have young children involved in your ceremony, make sure a parent or other guardian is close by at all times, just in case of tears or fears when it comes time to walk down the aisle. I always suggest having reserved seats (and parents nearby) for young children who are a part of the ceremony, as it is just too much (and can be too distracting) to require them to stand for the length of a ceremony.

what to wear

Your wedding attire, and that of your bridal party and guests, will vary depending upon the time of day and the formality of your celebration. Modern wedding fashions offer so many options for styles, materials, and details—the choices can seem endless and confusing.

STICKY SITUATION	SIMPLE STUNNING SOLUTION
I have more than one best friend. Choosing just one maid of honor would be impossible.	Lucky you! You can have two honor attendants and divide their duties.
A bridesmaid just told me she's pregnant.	No problem as long as she is in good health. Do keep a chair and a cool drink nearby in case she needs a break during the ceremony, and choose a dress she'll be comfortable in.
My fiancé's mother is insisting I make her daughter a bridesmaid, but I've already chosen my bridesmaids.	Just do it. Having one more maid is simply more love and support for you, and a happy mother-in-law-to-be has a lot of great benefits.
My groom doesn't seem interested in the wedding planning.	If your groom has limited time or interest in the fine details of the celebration, don't fret. Just speak with him about the things that are most important, and involve him in key meetings and decisions. It can be difficult for some grooms to sit through long discussions of color swatches and typeface styles, so it might be best to narrow down choices and select a few key options for, say, flower centerpieces, making a simple, straightforward presentation to your groom and asking for his opinion. Also, find out what subjects are most important to him (food? music?) and include him in fun activities like tasting the menu and listening to bands.

STICKY SITUATION	SIMPLE STUNNING SOLUTION
We are having a small wedding, but I want a big wedding party. Is that okay?	Well, in general, there should be more guests than attendants at a wedding ceremony! All joking aside, a good rule of thumb is a maximum of three attendants per side per one hundred guests. Of course, each situation is different, so just keep these guidelines in mind and do what's best for you.
We want a flower girl and ring bearer, but we really aren't inviting other children to the wedding. Do we need to invite our littlest wedding party members to the reception?	Yes. And you must invite their parents as well. If you think the children will tucker out or you'd prefer to have an adults-only reception, you can always provide a babysitter and a special "kids' room" with games, toys, and a comfy place to nap.

To help inspire you, here are some suggestions for bridal party attire, from casual daytime fashions to formal eveningwear. If you'd like more specific information on wedding fashion resources, see the Resource Guide (page 120).

(page 120)

> Let your choice of location and the spirit or mood of your wedding guide your selection of outfits and accessories. You'll likely want to dress less formally for a beach wedding than for a celebration in a fancy hotel or private club.

DAYTIME OR EVENING CASUAL

A casual wedding can be held any time of day, and it is often hosted as a barbecue or brunch at home or in a park or another informal location. You can really personalize your casual wedding attire to your wishes and needs, so feel free to add festive touches like flowers in your hair.

Casual bride She might wear a soft chiffon, silk, or organza dress; a chic linen suit; or a breezy gown. She might buy something off-the-rack or have a dress made for the occasion. Dress lengths for truly casual weddings tend to be ankle-length or shorter, but the bride can wear whatever she likes. Just make sure that you'll be comfortable in your dress, or if you want to wear a more formal gown for the ceremony, plan for a second, more casual outfit to change into for the reception.

If the bride wears a veil, it might be shorter in length, with a "blusher" in front that just covers her chin, but you can select what's best when you choose your dress. Some more casual brides prefer hats, which can be elegant and charming, but make sure that if you'll be married outside you have yours securely pinned to avoid fly-aways! Fresh flowers make pretty hair accents as well. Accessories would likely be simple and understated, and shoes could be pumps or sandals that easily slip off for dancing at the most relaxed celebrations. A casual bride might carry wildflowers, garden roses, or tropical orchids—something that suits the ceremony venue and her style.

Casual grooms There is a growing trend among grooms toward expressing a more personal style for wedding attire. I have seen grooms go tie-less in jeans and suede blazers; classically casual in khakis and sport coats; and totally laid back in lavender Vans and matching scarves. You should discuss, well in advance, what your fiancé plans to wear (from head to toe), so that he is both happy and coordinated with your ensemble. If he wants to be classically casual, warm weather suggests a linen, seersucker, or other lightweight suit or khakis and a blazer. He may want a flower for his lapel, or he may not even have a lapel. Just remember, it's his day too, and if he has an offbeat sense of fashion, that's probably one of the things you love about him!

Casual bridesmaids and groomsmen At a casual celebration, you may choose to let your attendants wear what they like, or you could coordinate outfits or accessories according to your wishes. If formal portraits are important to you, you might want to standardize outfits a bit (for example, there are many shades of little black dresses, so you might want to try them on together if matching is a priority).

For an outdoor wedding in warm weather, breezy skirts and tops or sundresses are always appropriate for the ladies, along with comfortable slippers or sandals. Men should take their cues from the groom, whether in jacket and tie or another ensemble, and shoes should be sandals or more casual dress shoes as opposed to the fancier, shiny varieties.

SEMI-FORMAL CELEBRATION

Most semi-formal weddings take place in the afternoon or evening, although for a daytime celebration, the same formula applies if you'd like your wedding to be a bit more dressy.

Semi-formal bride The bride's gown for a semi-formal event tends to be ankle or full length. It might be bias-cut satin (like the glamorous gowns of classic movie stars) or a more traditional A-line shape in silk or Duchesse satin, but typically for a semi-formal wedding, the bride will choose a gown with a less full skirt and a smaller train. Ball gowns (think fuller skirts and long trains) are generally reserved for the most formal weddings, but today, some brides are opting to wear the dress of their dreams even at less formal celebrations. Her bouquet might be a small, tailored gathering; a teardrop; or a looser, more ethereal design to complement her dress.

Semi-formal groom The groom at a semi-formal wedding would likely be in a tuxedo, with bow tie or classic long tie. If he prefers, a dressy suit in a style that flatters him is also appropriate, along with dress shoes in fine leather or patent leather. There are many wonderful options for fine men's clothing from off-the-rack designers, and certainly there are formalwear rental shops in almost every large town or city that can provide a variety of styles, along with alterations and other services. Traditionally, a semi-formal groom wears a boutonniere, or buttonhole flower, on his lapel, and this is a dapper detail.

Semi-formal bridesmaids and groomsmen Bridesmaids at a semi-formal wedding might be in long gowns or ankle- or knee-length cocktail dresses in chiffon, silk, satin, taffeta, or another fine fabric. Jewelry and accessories could be pearls, crystals, gold, silver, diamonds, or other stones with a more dressy feeling. Shoes might be sexy, strappy sandals, satin or leather pumps, or other elegant footwear.

Groomsmen at a semi-formal event will take their cues from the groom, as always, wearing tuxes if appropriate, or suits that coordinate with the groom's choice. Typically, for a semi-formal or formal wedding, the groom's attendants will wear closely matching attire—dark suits or three-button tuxedoes, black dress shoes, and matching ties.

FORMAL WEDDING

It is interesting to note that if you indicate "formal attire" on your reception invitation, gentlemen may wear dressy suits or tuxedoes. For the most formal celebrations, the wedding party is often in black tie, and sometimes, the invitation to the reception will note "black tie" to let the guests know a formal party is planned. These days, a reception would almost never call for "White Tie" attire (tailcoats and white ties for men), but it is possible for the men in the wedding party to be outfitted in white tie ensembles, with male guests dressed in black tie (tuxedoes or dark suits).

Formal bride She has many options to choose from among the gorgeous concoctions offered by today's best designers. The sky is truly the limit when it comes to details—and cost. There are sleek, minimalist designs, and dresses with stunning beadwork and vintage-inspired lace. Formal gowns might feature figure-hugging, couture-inspired shapes or the breezy softness of an empire waist. There are crystals and feathers and sashes and bustles—you name it! A formal bride wears a long gown, often with a full ball skirt and train. She might accent with a long veil in tulle or lace that sweeps behind her for the ceremony. Typically, the veil will be removed for the reception, and is sometimes replaced with a tiara or other hair accent.

Formal groom A morning coat, tuxedo, or tailcoat are appropriate attire for a groom at his formal wedding, depending upon the exact circumstances.

A morning coat (surprise!) is only appropriate for a wedding early in the day, and is gray or black and features a cutaway worn usually with striped trousers, vest, and ascot. A tuxedo is a formal suit (usually black, but a white jacket is also fabulously retro), worn with bowtie or long black tie. It should be worn only for weddings where the reception will begin after 6 P.M. A tuxedo or dark suit is appropriate for guests at a black-tie reception, and some modern grooms also opt for a dark suit rather than a tux.

A tailcoat (à la Fred Astaire) is only appropriate for the most formal evening weddings, and is considered white tie attire, although your invitation to the reception might read black tie, as most of your male guests will, perhaps sadly, not be prepared to sport tails and top hats. Gloves are traditionally worn with white tie, and can be a nice touch if the bride is also up for wearing gloves.

Formal bridesmaids and groomsmen Bridesmaids at a formal wedding can be dressed in short, fabulous cocktail dresses, long evening gowns, or tea-length creations with glamorous but elegant details. The objective is dressy and chic. Gloves are appropriate but not mandatory, and hair can be upswept.

The groom's attendants should coordinate their attire with the groom's, and if tailcoats are desired, they should be outfitted with matching ensembles by a good formalwear rental company to be sure the look is uniform and impeccable.

If your groom isn't particularly fashion-savvy, tear out photos from magazines of different styles of dressy attire and ask him what looks he likes. This will help focus the conversation and streamline the process of picking something perfect for him.

to wear white or not?

Anything truly goes these days for brides, although white and ivory are still the most popular choices. Champagnes, pinks, silvers, taupes, and pale blues are also in vogue, as are elegant dresses with prints and embroidery, even sashes and belts, in any color. Always think about your celebration and your personal style, and pick something that makes you feel special and beautiful!

Bridal Party Attire
DOS & DONTS

DO

▪ Will you marry in a house of worship? Make sure to speak with your officiant if your ladies' dresses feature bare arms or sexy details. You may want to provide shawls or wraps for the ceremony that can be taken off for the reception.

▪ Consider skin tone and body types when selecting dresses for your attendants. If you have a wide range of sizes and shapes, ensembles that offer variations on a theme might be your best choice, as you can customize each outfit with pieces that flatter every figure. You want your bridesmaids to feel wonderful and gorgeous!

DON'T

▪ Don't wait too long to choose and order your wedding gown or dress and outfits for your bridal party. With men's attire it's a bit easier, but bridal gowns and bridesmaid dresses can take up to twelve (or more) weeks to be delivered, and then you've got to have fittings and alterations. Of course, sometimes it's possible to pay a rush fee for faster service, but make the selection of attire one of your first priorities, and you'll save money and headaches.

▪ Don't be afraid to put your bridesmaids in black. Nothing is more flattering than a little black dress or a long, sleek black skirt, and often, this universal color is more wearable for other occasions in the future, so you might be doing your favorite ladies a favor by opting for dresses in onyx! Note that this tip applies mainly to formal or semi-formal celebrations.

▪ Don't forget to scuff your shoes before the big day. Same is true for brides, bridesmaids, and all the guys, as new shoes tend to be slippery. Use a nail file or sandpaper, and make sure to try them on—and leave them on—for at least an hour at least once before the wedding.

White is not off-limits—you can choose any style and color of dress that suits you and your celebration. The face-covering veil (or blusher) is still considered the first-time bride's prerogative, so unless you're into bucking tradition, a veil that is pinned to the back of the hair and trails behind is probably a better choice.

what about gloves?

Although in more glamorous times gloves were an essential accessory for every formal outfit (men's and women's), nowadays they are completely optional, but best saved for very formal events. Just remember, if you do wear them, you'll need to remove them for the ceremony and for the receiving line.

to buy or not to buy? a tux, that is.

The question of whether a groom should purchase a tuxedo all depends on how many formal events he'll attend each year. The rule is that if he finds himself at three or more formal evenings a year, it might be worth buying a tuxedo, as rentals will cost somewhere between a tenth and a third of the total cost of a new tux.

parents and grandparents

Chances are that your parents have a lot more experience getting dressed up than you do, and they may have strong opinions about the suggested attire at your celebration. Make sure to discuss your priorities with them so they'll fully understand your vision for the day, and listen to their advice and ideas before making your final decisions.

mothers of the bride and groom. wow!

Recently mothers have really stepped out of the shadows at weddings, putting together beautiful, unique ensembles that lay to rest the dowdy uniforms of the past. Designers are catering more and more to today's modern moms, offering suits, dresses, and gowns in flattering, attractive styles that give these special ladies a chance to shine on the big day.

fathers of the bride and groom

As with all the other gentlemen in the wedding party, fathers should generally coordinate their style and level of dress (suit, tuxedo, tails) with the groom's choice of apparel. A buttonhole flower is still very much in fashion for dapper dads, so be sure to include them in your floral order.

other non-guests at your wedding

Don't forget to think about (and discuss) what your service providers will wear at your reception. Will the band be in suits or tuxes? Do the waiters wear jackets and bowties? What about your photographer and videographer? Make sure you're happy with the attire arrangements for all your team members.

invitation ONLY

DESIGN, WORDING, AND ALL THE DETAILS

A wedding invitation is a very special piece of mail. After all, how often is it these days, in a world of email and cell phones, that we receive anything in the mail that is hand-lettered or beautifully printed? Every couple wants to create a unique and memorable invitation, one that will set the tone for the whole event.

But many of us have never written a formal invitation, nor have most of us been schooled in the art of how to choose papers, ink colors, font styles, or motifs. Inner envelopes, outer envelopes, tissue lining, letterpress, engraving—it's a lot to consider.

This chapter will guide you through everything you need to know to design and order your own perfect invitations. Let's start with the basics.

where to begin?

There are many and varied resources for invitations, depending upon your preferences, budget, and time frame. Start with a visit to a good stationery store, especially if you don't have much experience with printed materials. Locate a shop that advertises stationery or printing services, and ask to look at sample books for stationers they represent. You can place an order for your invitations directly through the store. This is a fairly straightforward process, and one of the more economical options for invitations, as designers have already created a line of styles that can be reproduced with your wedding details. You pick out an invitation format from the samples, and a salesperson helps you choose ink colors, typefaces, wording, and other elements such as calligraphy for the envelopes.

If you want something more customized, the options are truly endless, with artisanal letterpress studios springing up everywhere and graphic designers who can cater to your every whim. Tri-fold or booklet styles, vintage-inspired designs, invitations that resemble tickets or passports, even hand-calligraphed pieces that look like seventeenth-century love letters—anything goes! To locate a great designer, ask your venue or other wedding service providers for recommendations, or consult local bridal magazines or the Internet for resources in your area. See the Resource Guide (page 120).

Even if you do opt to go the more custom route, it's still a good idea to visit a stationery shop before your first appointment with a designer, as the experience of looking at styles and paper shapes and sizes will put you ahead of the game when communicating your wishes and needs for bespoke invitations. Remember that printing can take weeks or months depending upon your choices, so allow plenty of time to choose and refine details.

Of course the Internet also offers a lot of options for stylish, economical invitations, many of which follow the same format as those you might find in a good stationery store. The advantage: ordering online can be less expensive than visiting a store, and sometimes it's quicker. The disadvantage: you can't touch the sample papers or see ink colors in person right away (although you can often request samples by mail). To avoid surprises or disappointment, make sure to request paper and ink samples, as well as proofs (generally by email), before making your selections and giving your final approval.

cost factors

Wedding invitations fall into a wide range of budgets, and it helps to understand a bit about them before you begin the process of selecting elements and placing orders. There are three main things that contribute to the cost of anything that is printed.

PAPER

An overwhelming variety of paper sizes, shapes, and thicknesses are there for the choosing, and your selections will affect your overall printing budget. Most wedding invitations are printed on cardstock, and stock comes in numerous weights and textures. As a general rule, the thicker the stock, the pricier the paper. The same is true for unusual shapes and sizes of paper, even more so if they require special envelopes. Papers with special fibers or petals or other elements woven or pressed into the stock will also tend to be more expensive.

THE PRINTING PROCESS

There are numerous ways to print invitations, but most wedding invitations are printed by engraving or letterpress methods or by flat-printing methods like offset lithography.

- **Engraving** is the classic method for printing wedding invitations. If you were to run your hand over a piece of engraving, you'd find the text and other printed areas raised up off the page.
- With **letterpress**, the printed areas are recessed on the paper, so if you were to run your fingers over the type, you'd feel that the printed areas have been pressed right into the paper. Letterpress is a very popular printing method that can seem more artisanal and a bit less formal than engraving.
- A more economical choice is **flat-printing or lithography**, where the ink sits flat on the page. Most business cards and letterhead stationery are offset lithographed.

- Of course, with a **home computer and a laser printer**, you can create your own wedding invitations if you're so inclined. There are software programs for printing invitations available, and I've seen a number of graphically talented brides design truly beautiful pieces. The upside is that you've created something one-of-a-kind and personal. But don't be fooled—the cost (in time and materials) can end up rivaling some professional printing, especially if you add details like tissue lining or ribbons, and of course it's impossible to duplicate the textural aspects of engraving or letterpress if you're a fan of those styles.

DETAILS, DETAILS

Other elements that affect the cost of wedding invitations include the number of ink colors you choose (more colors are more expensive), as well as things like colored edging (which is sometimes done by hand), envelope styles and sizes, and whether you choose to line your envelopes or add ribbon or other details to the set. We'll talk below about what pieces each invitation set should include.

When you're thinking about your priorities (and your budget), take into account what's best for you. Visit a stationery store that specializes in printing invitations and ask to see samples of the various printing processes, so you can decide which you prefer.

set design

Invitation sets vary according to the circumstances of each wedding. A traditional wedding invitation set may include:

- An **outer envelope**, stamped and addressed with the names of each guest who is invited and printed with the return address on the back flap.
- The **invitation card** itself, sometimes tucked into an inner envelope which is addressed with the guest or guests' names only (no street addresses).

- A reply card with pre-addressed return envelope (or addressed on the reverse if a postcard is used).
- A separate **reception card** if the reception will take place in a location separate from the ceremony (although it is possible to print these details on the invitation itself, room permitting).

say it right

It used to be so easy. The bride's parents requested the honor of a guest's presence and everything pretty much followed from there. As family structures have changed, and with brides and grooms taking more of a role in hosting (and paying for) their celebrations, new ways of phrasing have become necessary. Choose one that's right for you, or craft your own unique wording. Here are some styles to get you started.

TRADITIONAL WORDING TODAY

This invitation wording invites all guests to the ceremony and reception, and assumes the bride's parents are hosting the wedding.

Mr. and Mrs. Donald Barton
request the honor of your presence
at the marriage of their daughter
Sophie Lynne
to
Mr. Jonathan Dean Thomas
Saturday, the sixth of February
Two thousand and ten
at five o'clock
St. Paul's Chapel
One Turtle Pond Road
Cincinnati, Ohio

And at the reception
immediately following the ceremony
Lakeside Country Club
Twenty-two Lakeside Place

But, of course, modern times have seen major changes in who hosts a wedding, and in whose names are included on the invitation. The main guideline is that whoever is paying for the majority of the wedding costs is considered the host, but your own situation may call for a unique approach. Here are a few variations on wording, based on style and circumstances.

BRIDE AND GROOM HOST THE WEDDING

This option is suitable whether the bride and groom are older, divorced, or simply paying for and hosting their own celebration.

> *Sara Aubrey Kuppin*
> *and*
> *Samir Dilip Chokshi*
> *request the honor of your presence*
> *at their marriage*
> *(or, as they exchange marriage vows)*
> *Saturday . . .*

INCLUDING THE FAMILY

This is the simplest way to include both the bride's and groom's families without listing names (which might involve divorced parents or other complicated combinations).

> *Together with their families*
> *Jennifer Catherine Leland*
> *and*
> *Robert Markham*
> *request the honor . . .*

FOR MORE FORMAL FAMILIES

If both sets of parents will host the wedding, it is lovely to include them both on the invitation.

> *Dr. and Mrs. Richard Bernstein*
> *and*
> *Mr. and Mrs. Lawrence Miller*
> *request the honor of your presence*
> *at the marriage of . . .*

Of course you can drop the honorifics for a less formal, more modern approach:

And if your mother goes by a professional or maiden name, you can certainly reflect that in your phrasing.

> *Laura and Richard Bernstein*
> *and*
> *Barbara and Lawrence Miller*
> *request the honor . . .*

KEEP INVITATIONS IN SYNC WITH YOUR CELEBRATION

Formal cardstock and phrases such as "The favour of a reply is requested" might not be the right choices for an informal ceremony and barbecue reception at home. Instead, opt for something along these lines.

> *Brittany Barrett*
> *and*
> *David James*
> *would be delighted if you would join them*
> *as they exchange marriage vows at home*
> *Saturday, the tenth of July*
> *Two thousand and ten*
> *1097 Bessmer Street*
> *Rhinebeck, New York*
>
> *The celebration continues with*
> *a backyard barbecue and hoedown*
> *under the starry sky*

reception cards

If the reception will take place at a separate location, it can be awkward to include those details (and another address) on the invitation to the ceremony, for reasons of space. A reception card made easy:

> *The pleasure of your company*
> *is requested*
> *at a reception immediately following*
> *the ceremony*
> *Spring Hill Country Club*
> *150 Heathertown Road*
> *Richmond, Virginia*

If there will be a gap in time between your ceremony and reception, let your guests know by indicating the time on your reception card. You can also note your requested attire:

The pleasure of your company
is requested
for dinner and dancing
at seven o'clock in the evening
The Old Mill
Two Miller's Hill Road
Ridgewood, New Jersey
Black tie

If the reception takes place on a different day than the ceremony, treat it like a separate invitation:

Leslie and Stephen Connor
request the pleasure of your company
for an evening of dinner and dancing
in celebration of the marriage
of their daughter
Madeleine
to
Nicholas Barton
Saturday, the Sixth of October
Two thousand and nine
six o'clock
Darcy Ballroom
New York City

ladies first

In general, the bride's family's names (or the bride's name) always come first on the invitation, and when the bride's parents are divorced, the bride's mother's name precedes the bride's father's name. Of course, if the bride's father is hosting the reception, his name would appear first, as would the groom's parents' names in the event that they are hosting.

commitment ceremonies and same-sex unions

The same etiquette guidelines for gay and lesbian celebrations apply as with any wedding invitation, taking into account the formality of your chosen celebration and your own preferences for naming the ceremony. Whether marriage, commitment ceremony, or celebration of vows, the same etiquette rules also apply to wording when it comes to who hosts the party, the date, and all the details.

your perfect wording

The fact is, you can and should customize your own wedding invitations to reflect your specific situation. You might be hosting a double wedding or a military wedding. You might have a deceased parent whom you'd like to honor on your invitation. There are too many variations to list them all here, but if you need more help with specific word choices for unique situations, speak with your stationer or see the Resource Guide (page 120) for more information.

how should guests reply?

One option is to print "RSVP" or "Please reply" on a lower corner of the invitation. If replies should be made to a phone number or to an address other than that on the back flap of the envelope, simply include that information:

> *RSVP (name and address or phone number of person accepting replies)*

Another more popular choice is to omit the "RSVP" text on the invitation itself, replacing it with a separate, postage-paid reply card included in the invitation set. This option, while more costly (as it requires a separate printed piece and additional postage), helps keep the invitation looking less cluttered and is designed to be convenient for guests. A reply card could take the form of a postcard or a small card with a pre-addressed and postage-paid envelope.

TRADITIONAL WORDING FOR A REPLY CARD

There are a number of lovely ways to phrase the wording on your reply cards. Can you believe that back in the day, there was no such thing as a reply card, and folks were expected to know how to craft a letter of reply on their own stationery?

But we must adapt to the reality of modern times and provide a convenient means of response for guests if we hope to hear back from them at all. The simplest is to include a small card with the invitation printed with a message such as "The favor of a reply is requested" or "Kindly reply by the fifth of June" and let your guests craft their own personal response to the invitation. But this option can create problems for guests who might forget to write their actual names on the card, and for hosts who read wonderful replies—"We can't wait! We'll be there with bells on"—but have no idea who wrote these sweet words.

An easier option for all concerned is to create a simple "form" for guests to fill in their replies, along with a target reply date, such as the following:

Kindly reply by the twelfth of May

M_____

will _____ attend

There are endless wonderful and appropriate variations for how to word your invitations. Discuss your special situation with your stationer or invitation designer, who will help you consider all the options.

No matter how you choose to word your reply cards, one trick of clever hosts is to number the back of the cards in pencil, just in case the guest forgets to write their name. The guest list coordinates to these numbered cards and provides a way to look up whose card is being returned, even if there's no name on it.

address for success

Addressing your envelopes is another important detail, for both practical and aesthetic reasons. In a formal wedding invitation, there can be as many as three envelopes. Here's a breakdown.

THE OUTER ENVELOPE

This is the mailing envelope that contains the entire invitation package. It may be adorned with a tissue lining or even sealed with wax. It is addressed (often by hand or in beautiful calligraphy) on the front side to the guest or guests invited. Remember, ONLY those guests listed on the envelope are invited to the celebration. The back of the envelope is typically printed with the return street address of the person hosting the wedding.

Example of how to address the front side of your outer envelopes:

Dr. and Mrs. Robert Jones
219 Fifth Avenue
Apartment 12
New York, New York
10018

Invitation
DOS & DON'TS

DO

- You must invite spouses and partners who live together. No exceptions. I recommend that you also seat them together at the reception.

- Proofread and verify all the details of your invitation carefully and have someone else you trust do the same. If printing addresses and phone numbers, dial them once before you approve your proofs, just to be sure.

DON'T

- Don't include dress-code information on a ceremony-only invitation. Only suggest a style of dress when the reception information is mentioned.

- Avoid printing restrictions ("Adults only") or information about the menu or bar ("Wine and Beer") on an invitation. Neither is appropriate or necessary.

- Never print registry information on your invitations.

- Don't invite guests as replacements for guests who decline. It's bad form. If you really need to have a second wave of invitations, make sure to send out the first wave early enough so that the second wave will receive their invitations no later than six weeks before the wedding.

- Don't assume people will say no. You'd be surprised how many people decide to accept wedding invitations, even when they live far away or are not particularly close to the couple. Never plan on more than ten percent regrets when estimating space and budgetary requirements.

- Don't print your wedding website on your invitation. It's fine on a save-the-date card, or you can let people know through friends and family or even an email. Some experts think it's acceptable to let guests reply to the wedding on your website. I know it seems easy, but it is just as easy—and much more polite—to write a quick reply on a card that is already stamped and drop it in the mail. A telephone call is the very minimum, in my opinion, in the spirit of staying connected at important occasions.

Of course you can change the format according to your wishes and needs. You can eliminate the honorifics (titles) before the guests' names and use the following style if you prefer:

Jessica and Robert Jones
219 Fifth Avenue
Apartment 12
New York, New York
10018

THE INNER ENVELOPE

It used to be customary to include an inner envelope, addressed simply with the names of the invited guests. More and more, in the spirit of less traditional invitations and a desire to save trees, couples are opting to eliminate this element. If you choose to have an inner envelope, simply follow the guidelines in the examples above, and list only the names of invited guests. Note "and family" on the line below parents' names if you want to invite all their children. If they have one young child, list the child's name under the parents' names. For older children (generally over 14 years of age), print a separate invitation just for them.

Richard and Celeste Carpiano
or
Miss Coleman and Guest
or
Errin and Justin Verdesca
Caitlyn Verdesca

good penmanship

You've probably heard of classic calligraphy. It's a form of artistic hand lettering, a beautiful throwback to the days when people actually practiced good penmanship. And it's fabulous. The thing is, fabulous often equals expensive, and calligraphy for mailing envelopes is generally charged per line, adding up to big bucks if your guest list is large.

Lately, some brilliant folks have come up with digital versions of gorgeous fonts to match all kinds of invitation styles. Because it's done by computer, it can be a lot less expensive, but the type of envelopes you're using will come into play, as some won't work with this process.

Is it amazing to have your envelopes hand lettered? Yes. Do I recommend it? Only if you don't have to go into debt to afford it. Otherwise, consider the digital option, or just hand-address your envelopes yourself, which is a beautiful touch.

get it together

If you'll order a set of stationery for your wedding, try to order multiple elements at the same time, as you may get a discount from your printer. Also, have your guest list in great shape in plenty of time to allow for addressing, stamping, and stuffing.

Envelopes
DOS & DON'TS

DO

- If you decide to omit formal titles, always list the woman's name first, as in the example above. This "ladies first" policy applies to escort cards as well, and to couples with different last names. The woman's name always appears first. Below is an example of how to address an envelope to an unmarried couple.

> Nadia Islam
> Amit Chatterjee

For a married couple with different last names, just add "and" after the woman's name. It's okay to have their names on two lines if necessary.

DON'T

- Don't abbreviate anything except formal titles such as Dr., Mr., and Mrs. Spell out state names (yes, even Mississippi), as well as words such as "Apartment," "Street," and "Avenue." You can use numerals for the apartment number or the exact street address:

> Dahlia Livingston
> 100 Old Palisade Road
> Apartment 3311
> Fort Lee, New Jersey 07024

tip

As a budget- and environmentally friendly alternative to an inner envelope, consider using a band of decorative paper to keep items together inside the main envelope. Also consider incorporating recycled papers into your designs.

STICKY SITUATION	SIMPLE STUNNING SOLUTION
Our good friends want to bring their children to our wedding, but we want to have an adults-only reception. How should we address the invitations so as not to offend anyone?	Only those people actually listed on the envelope are invited. If you receive a response for any guest you haven't invited (children or otherwise), you are correct to politely explain your priorities (e.g., small celebration, adults-only) and they are obliged by good manners to comply with total understanding.
We're having an informal wedding. Should we use titles like Mr. and Mrs. on our envelopes and invitations?	If your wedding is informal, skip the honorifics (e.g., Mr. and Dr.). For a more formal celebration (where your invitation itself would likely be more formal), they would be appropriate. Whatever your choice, remember to be consistent in all your printed materials (escort cards, place cards, and so forth).
People have been asking where we're registered. Should we print those details on our invitation or on a separate card?	You should not print those details at all. You should ask family and friends to spread the word. Alternatively, you can post registry details on a wedding website, with a link, as a convenience for your guests. If you're asked directly, feel free to share the details.
Our caterer wants us to include a menu option on our reply card. Is it appropriate?	Some wedding venues and catering facilities require exact counts for entree choices (e.g., beef, fish, vegetarian) in advance of the wedding date. I consider asking guests to select their entree for an event weeks in the future to be an unfortunate and outdated requirement, but if you are obligated to provide this information, you could include that on your reply card, worded politely.

Take a sample of your complete invitation to the post office and have it weighed before purchasing stamps. Make sure you plan for adequate postage, as you don't want these precious pieces coming back to you in the mail!

other printed materials for your wedding

On the way to your wedding, there might be numerous invitations to bridal showers, rehearsal dinners, and other events, and you'll find more information about those in the Satellite Celebrations chapter (page 79). But you also might want or need to consider some of the following elements for your big day.

IT GOES IN WAVES

Often, when you're working with a stationer or printer, there will be two (or even three) waves of wedding printing, depending upon the length of your engagement and your details. The first wave is generally for save-the-date cards and sometimes invitations. Then, as the date gets closer and plans for the ceremony and reception become finalized, there is often an order for programs and menu cards (if applicable), sometimes along with or followed by hand- or machine-calligraphied escort cards and place cards, table numbers, and other pieces.

CEREMONY PROGRAMS

A program conveys the order of the wedding service, sometimes lists the members of the bridal party, and might feature musical elements, such as the names of pieces and soloists. A program can also include readings, poems, quotes, or a message from the couple. Programs can take on almost any shape and format, from elaborate printed pieces in the shape of fans and booklets, to simple flat cards with basic information. They can be crafted at home or by a friend or printed professionally to coordinate with the other elements of the celebration.

I love programs, especially for ceremonies that involve unique or unfamiliar elements (as in a wedding that blends two traditions), but it has been my experience that these papers or booklets are often discarded immediately after the ceremony. If you'd like to have a ceremony program but you're on a budget or would prefer to keep your celebration more environmentally friendly, consider printing fewer programs and letting couples share. You can also order (or home-print) your programs on recycled paper.

WHAT THE HECK IS AN ESCORT CARD?

Escort cards are printed with guests' names and their table numbers, telling them to which table they been assigned. They can be classic flat cards in envelopes or folded "tent" cards, usually displayed at cocktail hour or the entrance to the reception. You can creatively combine your escort cards with guest favors by attaching personalized tags to a small box of candy or piece of fruit, hand-lettered keepsake bookmarks, or even candles!

PLACE CARDS

Place cards are used to indicate which place setting at a particular table has been reserved for a guest. You can use place cards at any style wedding, but they are best for very formal or very intimate weddings, or for weddings that feature long tables where seating might be confusing to your guests. Although they are a wonderful, thoughtful detail, using place cards requires a lot more effort on the part of the bride and groom, who must organize tables specifically and far enough in advance to write a card for each guest or to have them professionally lettered.

COMBINING PLACE CARDS WITH OTHER ELEMENTS

You can design a place card to work double duty. For example, if you will set a printed menu at every place setting, why not turn it over (or sideways) and have it lettered with the guest's name as a keepsake? I like to use smaller menu cards at the table, as they are less awkward for guests to manage.

If your seating configuration is complex or likely to change at the last minute, consider using a "card and envelope" format for your escort cards. This way, you can letter all the envelopes well in advance (go ahead and write an envelope for anyone you think might come—it will make life easier). Keep a little stack of numbered cards for each table number, and just stuff the envelopes with the number cards once your seating is firm. Then, if you have last-minute changes, you can simply open the envelope, switch the table number cards, and—presto!—you're the perfect host.

thank-you cards

You might want to have thank-you cards printed with your other wedding stationery. You can coordinate the design, and you might save a bit of money by adding them to the order. We'll talk more about the art of being thankful in the next chapter (see page 73), but here are some pointers for how to select or order the cards themselves.

You can of course buy lovely pre-printed thank-you cards, as long as there is enough blank space for you to write a personal note. Some couples like to have special, personal stationery for this aspect of wedding communication. Choose any size and style or color of card you like. Just remember, if you select a dark paper, you'll have to use a gel pen when writing your notes so the ink will show up.

Feel free to print both your names on the card and your home address on the envelope if you already live together. If you'll change your name after the wedding, your thank-you cards for gifts received before the wedding should feature your current name or monogram rather than your post-wedding name.

If you don't live together, you should have two sets of thank-you cards for gifts received before the wedding. Why two? Because grooms are now fully approved (and sometimes delighted) to participate in the thanking! So any notes he writes before the wedding should be signed by and issued from him.

post-wedding printing

See the Just Married chapter (page 113) for information on other printed pieces you might want to order before or after the wedding, such as at-home cards, monogrammed stationery, and wedding announcements.

yes, your wedding can be over-personalized

It's no secret that there are myriad resources available to couples today. Almost anything can be printed to coordinate with your celebration—buttons, wine labels, tissues, cocktail napkins—someone recently sent me a sample of monogrammed toilet tissue!

My advice is to use your judgment, and a little restraint, when it comes to "branding" your wedding with personalized products, so that the effect is beautiful and unique as opposed to just "everywhere." It's like pairing accessories with an outfit. You may have a giant jewelry box filled with great bracelets, earrings, and necklaces, but that doesn't mean you should wear them all at once.

printed items

STICKY SITUATION	SIMPLE STUNNING SOLUTION
We have couples on our guest list with different last names. How do we letter the escort cards?	Easy! Follow the same "ladies first" rule that applies to invitations. For couples with different last names, always list the woman's name first on the card, followed by the man's name. When you arrange your escort card display, alphabetize cards by the woman's last name as well. For same-sex couples, go alphabetically by last name.
We're having a buffet dinner. Should I print menu cards?	You certainly could print a card and put one at each place setting, or you could opt to print two cards and place them in the center of the table. Another option: print or write small, pretty cards to place on the buffet itself, identifying each delicious dish to make it easy for your guests to select their favorites.
We'd like to honor a family member who can't be with us. Should we put a note at the table?	A better choice would be to put a note in the ceremony program or to display a photo and a candle with a note on a small table near the entrance or guest book. You could also add a remembrance of loved ones to a blessing before your wedding meal.
Do we have to use titles, such as Dr. and Mrs., on our escort cards?	Titles are optional. They are a more formal choice and should be used when consistent with a more formal celebration.

please and THANK YOU

GIFT REGISTRY, FAVORS, AND ASKING FOR HELP

I used to be against the idea of registering for wedding gifts. To me, the concept that the gift receiver had a right to dictate what the giver should offer always seemed contrary to the whole notion of gift-giving. However, I have come to embrace wedding registry for reasons of sheer practicality and convenience for guests.

Many brides and grooms I speak with feel similarly awkward or ambivalent about signing up to ask for things, and it is definitely a subject where a solid grasp on gracious behavior is a necessity. Did you know that in Japan, newly married couples often present special gifts to their guests, in addition to throwing a party? Now that's hospitality.

You can register for almost anything, from classic place settings and kitchen utensils to couches and vacations and experiences. You can even register with a charity if you'd like to share your abundance with others.

Choosing where to register has gotten easier with more and more Internet sites dedicated to the huge business of wedding gifts. It's no longer necessary to pick just one store to register with—almost every national retailer (and many smaller ones) offer online wedding registry, where you can select all your gifts without ever leaving the house. But this incredible wealth of choices can be a bit over-the-top and sometimes frustrating. Here are a few things to remember about registering for your wedding and about gifts, and gratitude, in general.

Gift registry
DOS & DON'TS

DO

- Think carefully about your registry. If you're not the type to throw elaborate dinner parties every week, consider registering for a simpler china pattern you can use every day, rather than a fancy design you'll never take out of the cupboard. Don't register for gadgets you don't need. Focus on things you'll use and enjoy, not things you think you should have.

- Go registry shopping. Even if you register online, visit stores to look at items in person before choosing them. You'll save time, energy, and possible shipping or restocking charges by making sure you like what you pick.

- Choose items in multiple budget ranges. Be considerate of your guests' varying budget limitations and plan your registry accordingly. Most registries will keep you up to date on what has been purchased so you can add more items if necessary, and some vendors allow your guests to contribute to a larger group gift.

DON'T

- Don't print your registry details on your wedding invitation. Spread the word about where you're registered through friends and family. If you like, it is considered acceptable to put your registry info on a wedding website for the ease and convenience of your guests.

write thank-yous with genuine appreciation, and be specific

Mention the gift and how you plan to use it, whether it is an item from your registry, a certificate for services, a gift card, or a check. If you are sincerely thankful, this will show in your writing.

thank-you notes aren't just for gifts

For those folks who do lend their time, talents, or resources in support of the wedding, a hand-written thank-you note is a must. You may also wish to offer a small gift to those people who have done something special for you, whether it's hosting a wedding party in your honor, helping with wedding day transportation, or participating as readers during your ceremony. These gifts need not be extravagant—just something personal, offered with a lovely note expressing your gratitude.

> **tip**
>
> Keep a stack of cards and pre-stamped envelopes at home and another stack at the office and make it a point to send out a thank-you note before you throw away the wrapping paper or take a coffee break. If you can stick to this principle, I guarantee that you'll thank me later.

asking for help

While you're planning your wedding, you'll probably need help with a variety of elements, from running errands to taking care of out-of-town guests, to organizing transportation or setting up decorations. You might even just need some good advice or a shoulder to cry on in a stressful moment when it seems you have too much to do or too many things to think about. Your relationships with family and friends will dictate what's appropriate for you to ask, but don't be afraid to use your support network to make the process more enjoyable and less chaotic.

When you're considering whether to ask someone for help with a part of your wedding, large or small, keep in mind how your request will affect the

STICKY SITUATION	SIMPLE STUNNING SOLUTION
We can't seem to narrow our registry down to just a couple of stores. It seems we like just a few items from a bunch of places, but we don't want to overwhelm our guests with a list of different stores.	You're not alone. Check the Internet for websites such as www.myregistry.com that allow you to compile a single registry from multiple vendors.
We already have kitchenware, china, and bath towels. How should we register if we don't need these items?	You can register for unusual things, like travel, wine, or tickets to the theater. If you feel the desire to let your happy occasion benefit others, consider registering with a charity.
My fiancé and I are both really busy at work. Plus we're moving into a new house and planning the wedding. Can we just email a nice personal note to everyone instead of addressing envelopes and hand-writing notes?	No. You can certainly write an email of thanks if you like, but it doesn't count as a real thank-you note. The minute you tear open the gift wrap on that new copper cookware, you accept the responsibility to offer heartfelt, hand-written gratitude in return.
We are registering for donations to charity as opposed to gifts. Are we required to write a thank-you note to each person who makes a contribution?	Yes. And no form letter thank-you's, please. Take time to share a personal thought with the giver about why this cause is important to you, but don't let your tone become political or preachy.
What if we are late in writing our thank-you notes?	Write them anyway, no matter when.

person you're asking. For example, a young couple with a newborn baby might not be great hosts for your out-of-town guests, but an aunt and uncle with a spare room might be thrilled to open their home.

Make a list of things you'll need help to accomplish. Organizing it by time frame may be useful as the wedding day approaches. Whether it's preparing welcome gifts for out-of-town guests, picking up cupcakes, making sure Aunt Theresa has someone to drive her to the ceremony, an organized list helps you manage the many wedding-related tasks you'll need to address.

Tailor your requests for help to those for whom they're most suited, and you'll be much more likely to get the help you need. On the other hand, don't be offended if someone refuses your request for help. Although a reason might be offered, no explanation is necessary on their part, nor should you ask for one. Simply keep that request on your list and find another solution.

tip

You're only human. If you're feeling stressed out about the wedding, talk to someone you love—a parent, your best friend, a therapist! Remember that all the little details are wonderful, but they're just little details in the big, beautiful picture of your big day and your happy life. When you're celebrating something as wonderful as your own wedding, surrounded by loved ones and good friends, nothing else really matters.

satellite
CELEBRATIONS

WEDDING SHOWERS AND OTHER FESTIVITIES

We talked about engagement parties in the Rules of Engagement chapter (page 13), but there are a lot of other festive celebrations that surround a wedding.

There is one cardinal rule of etiquette related to all the parties that lead up to the big day. Never invite anyone to a satellite party who is not invited to the wedding itself. The only exception to this would be a bridal shower given by colleagues at the bride's place of employment.

wedding showers

These fun parties can be ladies-only or co-ed events. Traditionally they are hosted by someone who is not a member of the bride's family (since they are seen as occasions to "shower" the bride or couple with gifts, it could seem inappropriate for her family to host such a party). But it's really okay for any-one to host the shower, as long as it's not the couple themselves. Bridesmaids might co-host, or a group of close friends or even work colleagues might take on the responsibility. A shower is typically an informal affair, and the objective is to socialize, enjoy refreshments, and watch the bride (or couple) open gifts. Often there are activities or games.

Although it is lovely to send a printed invitation to a wedding shower, if it is a very small or very casual party, it is acceptable to invite guests by phone or even email.

From an etiquette standpoint, there are really only a few things to remember about a shower:

- The host must provide refreshments.
- You must open all your gifts at the party.
- Don't print registry info on the shower invitation. If you'll have a themed shower (e.g., bath, kitchen, lingerie), it is okay to note color preferences or sizes, and if the host wishes, she can include a separate note with the invitation specifying where you're registered.
- A thank-you note for a shower gift is required, even if you thank the giver in person at the party and even for gifts from people who don't attend the shower. A thank-you gift and note should be given to the host or hosts of the party by the bride or the couple.
- Everyone who is invited to the shower must be invited to the wedding.
- If you'd like more inspiration and ideas about how to host a fabulous wedding shower, take a look at the Resource Guide (page 120).

Celebration
DOS & DON'TS

DO

- Take time to enjoy these special parties and moments with your close friends and your families. Even though you are busy with work and planning a wedding, these are the moments you will really treasure.

- Be a considerate honoree. Remember to thank the host of any and every special event with a personal note and a small gift of thanks.

- Express your wishes regarding the size of each of your parties, special people you'd like to include, and any important details about things you really don't want, but do so politely and with consideration.

DON'T

- Don't take over the planning of your satellite celebrations. Let yourself be surprised and delighted by what your loved ones come up with for you.

- Don't make demands. If you have a request or an important priority, just let the hosts know politely and discreetly.

- Don't invite people yourself. If there's someone you want to include, ask the hostess if it's possible, and provide contact information.

bachelor and bachelorette fetes

This is an interesting topic for an etiquette book, as there are probably more breaches of "good" behavior that take place at these wedding-related events than at any other special occasion, and most of the time it's all in good fun.

But the fact is, many brides and grooms are asking their attendants to tone it down and plan something festive, fun, and more mature than what we typically think of for a bachelor or bachelorette bash. Dinner at a great restaurant, golfing weekends in Hawaii, spa days for the ladies—many businesses now cater to this growing market. Check out the Resource Guide (page 120) for more information.

What you choose is up to you. But as Judith Martin ("Miss Manners") puts it so succinctly, "If it's against state law, it's generally considered a breach of etiquette." The groom's and bride's attendants host these parties, and they should respect the honoree's wishes as to what kind of party they prefer.

bridesmaids' party

Sometimes brides (and traditionally their moms) host a luncheon, tea, cocktail party, or dinner to thank their attendants. This event usually takes place during the week before the wedding, in a restaurant or at the home of the bride or her family, and can be an opportunity for the bride to give her attendants a special gift and her sincere thanks for all their support.

groom's lunch

Hey, it's fine for the groom to do a little lunching with the guys if he likes. A groom's lunch could take place the week before the wedding or it could be a prelude to the wedding day festivities, held at home or in a restaurant or hotel dining room. It's a great time for the groom to share his thanks for the support of his wedding party, and it is also a perfect opportunity to give them small gifts of appreciation.

post-wedding parties

Sometimes parents or other relatives (or couples who have eloped or chosen small destination weddings) will wish to host a reception after the wedding. This party can be like any other wedding reception, but typically the bride and groom are not in formal wedding attire, and in most cases,

celebrations

STICKY SITUATION	SIMPLE STUNNING SOLUTION
My office mates want to throw me a shower. Do I have to invite them to the wedding? We're having a small celebration and my fiancé is not inviting work colleagues.	Don't worry. The rules of etiquette state that work colleagues may throw you a shower in support of the wedding, but that you are not obligated to invite all (or any) of your co-workers. You are obligated to write a personal thank-you note to everyone who has a part in creating your work shower and to everyone who gives you a wedding gift.
I am totally against my fiancé having a bachelor party. Should I just go out and have a wild bachelorette night in retaliation?	You should talk openly and with respect to your fiancé about this situation. Share your feelings with him and your concerns. You must build trust for your relationship to thrive, but only you two can determine what works for you in this situation. If he insists, send your brother along to keep an eye on him.
We want a very small wedding, so my fiancé's parents insist on hosting another party the week after the wedding for their friends. We were planning to leave right away on our honeymoon.	It would be really gracious of you to put off the honeymoon for a week to honor your new in-laws' wishes. Remember, this is a party in your honor, and the wedding magic continues! If you've already made reservations and risk losing a deposit, talk to your fiancé's parents about scheduling it for when you return, tan and well-rested.

traditions like cutting the cake and first dances should be eliminated. The host of the event takes care of all the details—invitations and replies, decorations, food, drinks, and so on. There may be toasts by the host and other key people.

the CEREMONY

BLENDING YOUR LOVE, TRADITIONS, AND BELIEFS

In almost every religion, the marriage ceremony is considered sacred and very special. Even in non-religious weddings, when two people open their hearts and promise to love and honor each other and share a life together, that moment is filled with hope, joy, and great meaning.

If you and your fiancé share the same religious affiliation, planning your ceremony may be as easy as speaking with your local clergy to determine which rituals and traditions will be included in your service.

However, if, like many couples today, you come from different traditions or cultures or you are not religious, you may find the idea of creating a ceremony that is personal yet respectful of both your beliefs and traditions to be a tall order. This chapter will help you by explaining some of the basics of religious and civil ceremonies. If you don't find what you need here, see the Resource Guide (page 120) for websites, books, and other sources of information and inspiration for your ceremony.

first things first

Talk about your ceremony together. Once you've announced your plans to marry, you'll want to think about where the wedding will take place. This may be an obvious choice, like a church or temple where you are both members, or it may require more thought if varying backgrounds or a desire to be married

Make sure it's official. Verify that your chosen officiant is authorized to perform weddings in your state. If you're hiring someone from an organization other than your local government or your house of worship, ask for documentation and references.

in a particular location will need to be taken into consideration. Spend some time discussing your priorities for the ceremony. This will help you determine where, when, and how you'd like to exchange vows.

You may find that your families have strong (and possibly differing) opinions about where you should be married. Remember to listen with an open heart, and always make an effort to be respectful, even if your beliefs differ from those of your family. Ultimately, your wedding ceremony should reflect who you are as individuals and as a couple, but if you desire, it is often possible to incorporate elements from your varying backgrounds.

Many religions permit interfaith marriages, and some will even allow dual officiants to participate in a wedding ceremony. You'll have to inquire with your own religious leaders to determine what works best for you.

If you or your partner are members of a religion that frowns upon interfaith marriages, you may decide to have two separate ceremonies, or to hold a civil ceremony, led by a non-religious officiant such as a judge, mayor, or city clerk.

Once you've talked about your preferences and wishes for the ceremony, make sure to do your research. Investigate state and local regulations for any required health tests and to obtain your marriage license. The Internet is a great resource for this type of information—just visit your local government's website and search "marriage" and, if applicable, make an appointment to speak with your clergy or a religious representative as soon as possible after your engagement.

christian ceremony basics

Wedding ceremonies in various branches of Christianity (Catholicism, Protestantism, and so on) will differ in numerous ways, but there are many similarities. Below is a general overview of a Christian ceremony, from processional through recessional.

Keep in mind that many churches require religious preparation or counseling prior to the ceremony, and some even have restrictions on who may be married within the church, especially with regard to interfaith weddings and ceremonies where one or both partners have been married before. The Catholic church, for example, does not recognize divorce, so it would likely be impossible for a divorced Catholic whose first marriage was performed in the church to remarry within the church. Make sure to check with your local religious authority to find out everything you need to know.

THE LINE-UP

In a typical Christian ceremony, after all the guests are seated, the mother of the groom is escorted to her seat in the first row on the right side of the aisle as you face the altar. Next, the bride's mother is ushered to her seat in the front row on the left side of the aisle. This is the signal that the ceremony is about to begin.

If there is an aisle runner, the ushers or other appointed folks pull it now. The music is cued and the officiant enters (typically from a side vestibule) with the groom and the best man. Sometimes all the groomsmen accompany the groom, although the groomsmen might also escort the bridesmaids down the aisle. Also, some grooms prefer to walk down the aisle. Just check with your clergy to find out what's possible.

Typically groomsmen and bridesmaids process in order so that those who are first down the aisle stand farthest away from the bride and groom. Bridesmaids stand on the left side, while groomsmen stand to the right. Some traditions provide for all or some of the wedding party to be seated during the ceremony.

Just before the bride's entrance, the maid or matron of honor processes, preceded or followed by the ring bearer and the flower girl, either separately or in pairs. It is advisable for small children to be seated with their parents or a guardian once they've made their walk down the aisle, and someone should be on hand just in case of a mid-procession meltdown.

If the bride is accompanied by her father or another escort, she walks on his left side and is received by the groom at the end of the aisle. Some Christian ceremonies provide for a "giving away" of the bride, after which time the bride's father or escort is seated next to the bride's mother on the left side of the aisle.

SAYING I DO

In a Christian ceremony, there is often a welcome or call to prayer, followed by readings, vows, and the exchange of rings. Rituals and traditions within the ceremony will vary from branch to branch. For example, a Catholic service might include a mass with Holy Communion, or it may be a more abbreviated service. Some Christian services include a sermon, while others don't. The ceremony generally ends with a pronouncement ("by the power vested in me, I now pronounce…") and a kiss.

The recessional for a Christian wedding is simply the processional in reverse order, with the newly married couple in the lead. Immediately following them, the flower girl and ring bearer might join in the walk back up the aisle, followed by the honor attendants and the bridesmaids and groomsmen in pairs. Parents follow the last members of the wedding party, after which guests are free to leave their seats.

jewish ceremony basics

Again, depending upon your branch of Judaism (Orthodox, Reform, and so on), rituals and traditions will vary, as will positions on interfaith marriage and other details. It is important to seek guidance from your religious leaders to determine what is possible (and what is required) for your Jewish ceremony.

PRE-CEREMONY TRADITIONS

There are several traditions that take place just before the start of a Jewish wedding ceremony. The most common is the signing of a ketubah, or marriage contract. Some couples choose to display this beautiful document during the reception.

Other pre-wedding rituals include the groom's tish, or table, where the groom gathers with male friends and family before the ceremony, and the bedecken, or veiling, of the bride by the groom.

One of the most wonderful traditions of a Jewish ceremony is that of the huppah. A huppah is a simple structure, typically four poles and a canopy, meant to symbolize the beginning of the couple's new life together. The couple will take their vows under this canopy. The huppah can be hand-carried by close friends or family, or it can be a structure that is in place before the ceremony begins, decorated with fabric or flowers. You should check with your rabbi before planning the decor for your huppah, and the idea should be to keep this symbol of your new beginning simple, rather than going over-the-top.

THE LINE-UP

Again, traditions will vary according to your branch of Judaism, but here's a general outline of a Jewish wedding processional. When it's time for the ceremony to begin, the music may be cued. The first people down the aisle are the rabbi and, if applicable, the cantor. They take their places under the huppah. Immediately following them are the bride's grandparents, followed by the groom's grandparents. Grandparents are typically seated for the ceremony.

In a Jewish wedding, the bride's side is the right side, so the bride's guests might be seated along the right side of the aisle, facing the huppah, while the groom's family and friends might be seated along the left side of the aisle.

Next come the groomsmen, typically walking in pairs, followed by the best man. These gentlemen take their places to the left side of the huppah (as you face the huppah), with the best man nearest where the groom will stand.

The groom makes his entrance, generally accompanied by both of his parents, with his dad on his right and mom on his left. Some couples ask their parents to stand up under the huppah for the ceremony, while others prefer them to be seated.

After the groom, the bridesmaids come down the aisle single file or in pairs. The maid or matron of honor follows them, and all the ladies take their place on the right side of the huppah to await the bride.

If there is a flower girl or ring bearer, they make their entrance now, just before the bride. It is advisable to save a seat for any of these young members of the wedding party, rather than asking them to stand, and when young children are involved, you should have a family member on hand to receive or assist them if the need arises.

The bride enters, traditionally accompanied by her father to her right and her mother to her left. There is often a special piece of music to signal her entrance. Once down the aisle, the bride is received by the groom, and the ceremony begins.

SAYING I DO

A Jewish ceremony may begin with an ancient ritual of circling, where the bride walks around her intended seven times, signifying that he will be the center of her world. Some modern couples circle each other, but check with your rabbi to determine what's best for you.

Other elements include the betrothal, or kiddushin, where the couple takes sips from a cup of wine and receives blessings before the groom places a ring on the bride's right index finger (considered to be a direct connection to her heart). In some ceremonies, the bride also offers a ring to the groom. The rabbi may read from the ketubah as well, and the seven blessings may be read in Hebrew and English by the rabbi, or by friends and family.

The ceremony ends with the "breaking of the glass," where the groom stomps on a glass wrapped in a napkin or special bag to symbolize the destruction of the temple at Jerusalem and the vulnerability or fragility of life. At this point, the crowd shouts, "Mazel Tov!" and the celebrating begins.

The recessional at a Jewish wedding is basically just the reverse of the processional, except that the men and women, in some cases, pair off to exit in couples. The bride and groom are first back up the aisle, followed by the bride's parents, the groom's parents, the bride's grandparents, then the groom's grandparents. The flower girl and ring bearer may join the recessional as well, and the honor attendants come before the maids and groomsmen.

other religious ceremonies

If you would like more information on religious ceremonies not included in this chapter, please see the Resource Guide (page 120) for links to helpful books and websites.

interfaith ceremonies

Depending upon your faiths and your previous marital status, you may be able to have a religious interfaith service, either in a house of worship or in a civil setting, such as in a loft or party space or on a beach. You'll want to do your research and speak to your religious advisors to find out what's possible. For resources on interfaith marriages, take a look at the Resource Guide (page 120).

civil ceremony basics

A civil ceremony can take place almost anywhere you can imagine—in a courthouse, on a mountaintop, at the beach, or in your own backyard. A civil ceremony may or may not include elements from religious or cultural traditions, and may include a processional and recessional, or may be much more informal.

Civil ceremonies can be entirely non-religious, but often follow a format similar to a religious wedding. Welcoming remarks, vows, rings, a pronouncement, and a kiss are elements of many civil ceremonies.

This type of ceremony can be less restrictive than some religious services, and can offer a great opportunity to personalize with readings, music, and other details such as vows written by the couple.

same-sex ceremony basics

The debate over legalizing same-sex ceremonies (and over sanctioning them religiously) continues to rage, leaving many committed couples who wish to join their lives together looking for meaningful ways to seal their union.

A gay or lesbian couple wishing to hold a commitment ceremony should approach the celebration itself much in the same way as any couple wishing to marry. Although at this time a marriage license may be impossible to obtain, if one or both of you are religious, a conversation with your clergy is a top priority, as differing religions have varying positions on the subject. Some religions offer ceremonies to acknowledge or bless the union, while others don't. Depending upon your beliefs and your individual situation, you'll decide whether a religious blessing or a civil ceremony is right for you.

blending your cultural traditions

Incorporating your heritage and cultural history into your wedding ceremony (and reception for that matter) is a fantastic idea. In many Eastern traditions, brides and grooms feed each other sweets during the ceremony to symbolize their sweet future together. Indian brides and grooms exchange flower garlands, and one beautiful Hindu tradition asks married women to whisper good wishes in the bride's ear during the ceremony. African-American brides and grooms sometimes jump over a decorated broom in honor of their enslaved ancestors who were not permitted to marry. Find out what special elements brides and grooms of your heritage include in their ceremonies.

Ask your parents and grandparents to share ideas with you if you need inspiration, and consider incorporating traditional music or readings from beloved writers or poets as a way to layer your ceremony with multi-cultural details.

- In a Greek wedding, for example, gold or silver crowns joined by ribbons are placed atop the heads of the bride and groom, and exchanged throughout the ceremony. At the reception, guests dance in a circle, plates are shattered and money is tossed for good luck.
- Hindu brides and grooms step on seven piles of rice as they recite seven vows relating to their families, their home, and their new life together. The whole community joins in as all the married women in attendance are invited up to the mandap (wedding canopy) to whisper best wishes into the bride's ear.
- Filipino couples select other married couples to act as sponsors. There are typically several sets of sponsors who participate in the ceremony, joining in a prayer and blessing for the couple as they take their vows. "Unity coins" are also brought to the altar by sponsors, to symbolize prosperity and the couple's mutual contributions to the marriage and family.
- A Swedish bride wears coins in her shoes—a gold one given by her mother and a silver one given by her father—to symbolize that she will always be taken care of.
- In Ireland, brides often braid their hair on their wedding day, as it's considered good luck.
- In Portugal, couples traditionally visited each of their wedding guests the day after the celebration to thank them for sharing in the beginning of their new life together. And you thought writing thank-you notes was a lot of work!

writing your own vows

Some couples prefer the structure of a ceremony that includes traditional vows, while for others, the idea of creating personal vows is appealing and unique. Discuss your wishes with your officiant, and if you decide to write your own vows, make sure you take the time to discuss them with your spouse-to-be, and allow yourself plenty of time to work on them.

Keep your vows succinct and heartfelt, adding a few details that illustrate your love story in a personal way. Avoid anything that's a private joke or otherwise not inclusive, and keep humor minimal and charming. Practice your vows before the ceremony to make sure they sound out loud the way you intend them, and to help ease your nerves. Sometimes emotions can be overwhelming the first time you speak such meaningful words, so a little practice can help your composure.

choosing readings

There are numerous books and many resources on the Internet to help you find poetry, quotes, or readings you might wish to include in your ceremony. Just search "wedding readings." If you'll be married in a religious service, ask your clergy for guidance in choosing appropriate material. If you have a friend or family member who is a poet or writer, inquire with your officiant as to whether you might be able to include such a reading in your ceremony.

In general, keep readings short, meaningful, and inclusive. If you'll read from a passage or poem that is less well known but special to you as a couple, ask the reader to introduce the reading with a brief explanation of why it means so much to you.

If you'll be reading your own vows or if members of your wedding party will need to refer to a reading during the ceremony, it's a great idea to print it out double-spaced, in slightly larger type size. Nervous readers can lose their place, so this little trick can be a big help.

ceremony programs

A wedding program can be a single page listing the bridal party and a brief order of the service, or it can be a folding card or a multi-page booklet that might include readings, descriptions of wedding rituals or traditions, even notes of thanks from the bride and groom. You can print programs on a home computer or have them custom-designed by your stationer to match your other wedding materials, complete with monograms or other motifs and details.

Because, sadly, programs tend to get discarded at the end of a ceremony, I suggest keeping them small in size (so that they might fit in a man's jacket pocket) and printing just enough to give one to every couple rather than every single individual. This will save you in printing fees, and might even save a tree, which is always a good thing.

STICKY SITUATION	SIMPLE STUNNING SOLUTION
We're not sure how to seat guests at our ceremony. Do we have to have a bride's side and a groom's side?	Traditionally, in Christian weddings, the bride's family and friends sat in the pews or rows on the left side of the aisle facing the altar. In Jewish weddings, the bride's side was the right side. Nowadays, many couples opt to forego "sides" and just seat guests as they arrive in the best possible seats.
How do we make sure seats are saved for our immediate family and readers?	In the old days, important guests were often given a card reading, "Within the ribbon," admitting them to the first few roped-off rows. An easier and more personal option is to place cards or signs with the names of important guests on the seats in your first few rows. Just make sure to let the appropriate folks know in advance that you've saved seats for them, and review your seating plan with ushers or your coordinator.
Not everyone in our wedding party can make it to our rehearsal. We're not even sure if our officiant will be there. What should we do to make sure everything runs smoothly?	It is not uncommon for a wedding party to rehearse without the officiant or even without a member of the wedding party. If your officiant won't be able to rehearse with you, use your program or a written outline as a guide, and ask a trusted friend or your wedding coordinator to lead the rehearsal. If you'll rehearse on the big day, and you don't want to see each other, it's okay for the bride not to rehearse. After all, once she makes it to the end of the aisle, her groom will be there to receive her!

STICKY SITUATION	SIMPLE STUNNING SOLUTION
Our families and backgrounds could not be more different, but we want to bring our unfamiliar traditions together. How can we make everyone feel included in our ceremony?	If possible, incorporate traditions from both of your heritages. Consider printing a program that describes unfamiliar rituals so your guests will understand the beauty and meaning of what is taking place. And set aside a time well before the big day for your families to meet and bond.
My father, whom I haven't seen in years, will attend the wedding, but I want my stepfather to walk me down the aisle. My father is pressuring me. What to do?	You should be escorted by whomever you wish. Just put on your diplomat hat and explain your wishes to your father honestly but in the most respectful way possible. It is his obligation to understand and respect your decision.

receiving line—yes or no?

A receiving line is a formal tradition that requires a chunk of time either immediately following the ceremony or at some point near the beginning of the reception. A lot of gracious parents still think it's a good way to make certain all guests have been greeted formally, but many couples these days don't want to sacrifice their cocktail hour to stand in line, and prefer to greet their guests personally, table by table, at the reception.

If you'd like to have a receiving line, here's what you need to know. Typically, the receiving line starts with the two pairs of parents (or at least the moms—dads sometimes prefer to work the room). Following them is the happy

Ceremony
DOS & DON'TS

DO

■ Explore regulations, requirements, and options before designing your ceremony. Some houses of worship have very specific guidelines, and some require in-house printing of wedding programs and approval of all wedding music. Others prohibit or restrict photography, videography, and even floral arrangements and aisle runners for the ceremony.

■ Ask for a written confirmation of your ceremony time, and make sure you've allowed for any special considerations, such as taking wedding portraits after the service or hosting a receiving line. Remember there may be other celebrations or services going on before or after your ceremony.

■ Appoint someone to collect your precious ceremony objects. This could be an usher, a friend, or your wedding planner.

DON'T

■ Don't forget to invite your officiant (and spouse if applicable) to the reception. If they accept your invitation, seat them in a place of honor, preferably away from loud music and "party people." If they decline, don't be offended—it's no reflection on your wedding, and you've done your duty as a gracious host.

■ Don't underestimate the value of a brief pre-wedding rehearsal. Even for a small wedding party, a rehearsal can help calm nerves and make things run more smoothly on the big day. Ask your house of worship or your ceremony venue if a rehearsal the day before is possible, and if so, ask for a written confirmation of the date and time. If you can't rehearse in the actual ceremony location, don't worry. Just simulate an aisle and your vow space and give everyone a chance to practice the processional and take their positions. Also, let folks practice walking back up the aisle in reverse order so they'll feel comfortable when it's time for the recessional.

couple, the maid of honor, and sometimes the bridesmaids. It's important to keep the line moving with a sincere handshake or kiss and a heartfelt thanks for coming, while avoiding long conversations that might keep guests waiting even longer. You can estimate about five to six guests per minute on average, so a hundred-person wedding will take about twenty minutes of your time.

If your ceremony is short and sweet, a receiving line can be a nice way to share your newlywed joy with family and friends. If you're having a lengthy service, you may decide to forego the receiving line in favor of a quicker transition to the reception, especially if you'll need time for portraits with the wedding party between the ceremony and the reception. But remember, your parents are right about one thing: it's important to find a moment to speak to each and every guest at your wedding, and to thank them for sharing this amazing experience with you. After all, they've just witnessed one of your life's most precious occasions.

tip

It's important to check with your ceremony venue to make sure a receiving line is possible from a timing standpoint. If there is another service following yours, or if your ceremony venue needs to be transformed into your dining room while you're at cocktail hour, it may not make sense to eat up precious time with a receiving line.

PERFECT
party

Ask your mother. Many wedding receptions at one time were informal gatherings in the community room of a house of worship or at a family home. Following the ceremony, the cake would be cut and champagne would be offered with a toast or two.

At more formal celebrations, a wedding feast might be served, sometimes with dancing, but with a very structured format that became rather formulaic in its inflexibility.

These days it's all about personalizing the celebration, and couples are putting their own unique stamp on their parties with details such as personalized musical playlists, vegetarian menus, and cocktail receptions instead of seated dinners.

You can have any kind of wedding reception you like, but first you should know what to consider when planning the structure of your party. Here we'll touch on some of the main elements and traditions of a wedding reception, and you can decide which combination is right for you.

what kind of reception?

The two most popular types of wedding receptions today are a seated dinner (with food served at table or from a buffet) and a cocktail reception with smaller nibbles, drinks, and wedding cake or dessert.

SEATED DINNER

A seated reception is the classic format of recent times. Guests typically enjoy a cocktail hour (of forty-five minutes to an hour and fifteen minutes) with hors d'oeuvres, during which time they take an escort card to find out where they're seated for dinner.

As stated above, dinner might be served at the table or at a buffet. The meal is often accompanied by dancing (before or after dinner), toasts, and a cake cutting.

- **Why Yes:** Classic, traditional, more formal, great for moments like speeches.
- **Challenges:** May be too traditional for some couples.

For a seated dinner served at table, here are some options that work well.

- **Plated service** Waiters present finished plates of food for each course. For a wedding, this is generally three courses—appetizer, entree, and dessert. Wedding cake may represent the dessert, or it may be served separately.
- **French service** In this style of service, waiters finish dishes at the table-side or serve each guest from large platters. This can be easier from the kitchen standpoint, but may require extra waiters to expedite this very hands-on service. Also, the finished plate will not be as beautifully composed as if a chef creates it in the kitchen.
- **Russian service** This is similar to French service, in that large platters are brought to the table. But Russian service is slightly less formal, as guests help themselves while waiters hold the trays.
- **Family-style service** This is the most informal, and perhaps most convivial option, wherein waiters place platters of food in the center of every table, with guests passing the platters and helping themselves. If you choose this option, ask for small platters that will be easy for your guests to pass amongst themselves.
- **Buffet-style service** Food is arranged in large portions on buffet tables. Guests are invited to visit the buffet to help themselves. If you choose this

style of service, make sure there are staff members on hand to maintain and replenish buffets, as well as to explain ingredients in each dish. Ask whether there are chic alternatives to the standard old "chafing dishes." Many savvy caterers have devised gorgeous presentations to make buffets beautiful. Also, arrange for waiters to pour wine and clear and reset silver as necessary throughout the meal.

COCKTAIL RECEPTION

This less traditional reception is becoming more and more popular with couples who don't want a "weddingy" wedding. They are mavericks who don't want a roomful of guests sitting down for hours to eat. These receptions are anywhere between two and five hours long, and they may involve passed hors d'oeuvres and sweets only or more elaborate "tasting stations" to provide a bit more sustenance.

Although some seating should be provided for elderly folks or those with less mobility, most guests will stand and mingle. Often there is a DJ or an electronic playlist rather than a live band.

- **Why Yes:** Edgy, fun, chic, elegant, different.
- **Challenges:** For a larger group, it can be difficult to organize people for moments like toasts and cake cutting.

seating

If you will have a seated dinner, you'll have to think about who sits with whom. Let's start with the bride and groom. The tradition of a dais, or raised platform, where the bridal party faces all the wedding guests has become much less popular in favor of tables set among the guests.

Also falling out of favor is the notion of the "sweetheart table," a small table set for two, so that the bride and groom sit alone. This tradition might have arisen as a result of the fact that many newlyweds barely sit during their receptions, always getting up to greet their guests, dance, and cut the cake.

Many couples today choose to sit at the reception with the members of their bridal party, while their parents are seated with each other or separately, each set of parents hosting a table of their respective friends and family. Here are some things to keep in mind when you're planning your seating.

STICKY SITUATION	SIMPLE STUNNING SOLUTION
We're having a seated dinner, but we want it to be less stuffy. Do we have to assign seating?	Unless your wedding is very small and very casual, you should create a seating plan that assigns each of your guests to a particular table. It is thoughtful and considerate to make sure everyone has a seat. If you do not assign tables, you risk empty seats or guests who can't sit together.
What can we do to prevent all our guests from stampeding the buffet at the same time?	I recommend having your waiters invite guests graciously, table by table, rather than making an announcement of any kind.

Seat elderly people farther away from the band or speakers. Position yourselves in a highly visible location, making sure you aren't hidden behind a pillar, post, or tent pole.

Even if you don't use place cards on other tables, provide them for the bridal table so that it will be clear where you wish to sit. When arranging the tables, be mindful of people who might not wish to sit together and do your best to find a place where each will be comfortable.

HOW DO WE ARRANGE OUR HEAD TABLE?

You can create a seating plan at your bridal table that suits your needs and wishes. The size of your bridal party will likely affect your seating, and you should include spouses of attendants at your table if space permits.

In general, bride and groom are seated next to one another (tradition-ally, the bride was seated at the groom's right), in a central location, near the dance floor if applicable, and facing the area where speeches will take place.

As far as who sits next to whom, or who should be included, here are a few tips:

- Parents can be seated at your table, but today parents often host their own tables near the head table. If there are young children in your bridal party and you want to include them at your table, make sure you allow seats for their parents as well.
- If your officiant will be present at your reception (and they must be invited), seat them in a place of honor, either at your head table if you are sitting with your parents, or at a parent table. If there is another group with whom your officiant would be most comfortable, feel free to make accommodations.
- Arrange place cards at your head table, even if you aren't using them anywhere else. This will make it clear where you'll be seated.

welcoming guests

As mentioned previously, assigning your guests to particular tables is highly recommended for all but the most casual receptions. It is thoughtful and will make everyone feel more at ease.

If you've chosen not to have a receiving line after your ceremony, the entrance to dinner can be another opportunity for you to greet guests. A receiving line, as mentioned before, has its pros and cons to consider. It's a

As guests enter the reception, make sure there are staff members in place with seating charts in hand to help your friends and family find their seats and to answer any questions they might have. Little details like this are the mark of a polished party.

lovely tradition, where the newlyweds stand with their parents (or just their mothers) and the maid of honor. Bridesmaids are sometimes included but typically not children (unless they are the children of the newlyweds and wish to participate) or the groom's attendants. A receiving line can be a great way to make sure you've greeted all your guests, especially at a large wedding (more than one hundred guests), but it will typically take at least twenty minutes, so you should think about all the details of your timing and determine whether it's right for you.

Typically, the receiving line goes in this order: bride's mother or parents, groom's mother or parents, bride, groom, maid of honor, and bridesmaids.

Also to be considered are your family dynamics. If you have divorced parents or any other set of circumstances that would make a receiving line awkward, you might want to reconsider, or design your receiving line with you between sets of parents.

announcing the bride and groom

You may wish to be announced as you enter the reception. This is a festive tradition to "introduce" you to your friends and family as husband and wife. More and more, couples are foregoing the loud, cheesy fanfare and parade of bridal attendants in favor of a more elegant announcement of the bride and groom only.

If you like the idea of an announcement but want to keep it simple and sophisticated, instruct your bandleader or DJ to wait until all your guests have been seated for the meal, making a simple, elegant introduction: "Ladies and gentlemen, please welcome the newlyweds, Laura and John." Of course, if you prefer the more formal, "Mr. and Mrs.," that's just fine too. You may choose to follow this moment with your first dance, or you might prefer to just walk to your table and be seated for dinner.

In the classic wedding dinner format, dance sets are sometimes interspersed between meal courses. But the tide is changing. Now, dinner before dancing is becoming a more popular idea with brides and grooms who want everyone to sit and share a meal before cutting a rug. The advantage to this is that the meal flows more quickly, and you can focus on speeches and socializing before the dancing begins, and then really kick off the party.

> If you want your announcements to be made in a certain way, give your bandleader or DJ a script for the evening, with specific wording for any announcements or introductions. Note whether or not you'd like music played for these introductions, and be clear about your wishes to avoid any surprises at the party. Make sure to explain the relationship of each person who might be introduced for toasts or other moments to avoid confusion or hurt feelings.

music at your reception

So many brides and grooms tell me that they consider music to be one of the most important elements at their parties. It's true—music creates mood. Here are a few tips to help you in designing music that will be pleasing to both you and your guests.

Seat older guests away from loud music. Check your site for speaker positioning, as some venues will have speakers in unlikely places.

Your wedding is not the time to share your encyclopedic knowledge of little-known songs. If you want people to dance, focus mostly on music people know. Swing, jazz, and American Songbook classics for the older folks, disco and eighties music for the middle generations, and current pop and dance tunes for the younger set. If you really need to hear your unusual music at the wedding, play it on a CD or iPod at a low level during cocktail hour.

Play soft background music at dinner. This allows guests to talk while they dine, and gives the older folks a break from loud dance music.

If you hire a big band for the reception, ask if you can "borrow" a few musicians for a cocktail hour trio or quartet.

toasts

Wedding toasts are a wonderful tradition. What could be better than hearing people you love sharing heartfelt good wishes for your happy future? Here's what you need to know.

Traditionally, the best man gives the first toast, but these days this is sometimes preceded by a welcome from the bride's parents, and a response from the groom's parents. When it comes to wedding toasts, the best advice is to keep them simple, sincere, and short. And always in charming good taste.

Ideally, there should be as few toasts at the wedding as possible, and they should take place during or between dinner courses, in groups of no more than two to three at a time. If you have a lot of friends who want to toast, open the microphone the night before the wedding at the more casual rehearsal dinner. Even then, however, toasters should still keep it short.

Many brides and grooms want to say a few words at their reception. A perfect time to do this is just before or after the cake cutting, when your guests

Here's something not a lot of people know. When someone is toasting to you, you don't raise a glass or drink to yourself. In the past, guests were expected to stand for each toast, but that tradition has fallen by the wayside. Now, the toast-maker stands, usually in a central location, and at the end of the speech, the bride and groom often rise to share a hug or handshake with the speaker.

will be gathered around you. Again, keep it brief and sincere, looking around the room to include all your guests, and looking directly at each other when you're speaking to one another. You might choose to write something special to ensure you get the words out just the way you want.

photography and videography

Discuss your wishes and preferences with your chosen photographer and videographer to ensure that you and your guests have a positive experience at the reception. If you prefer that guests not be asked for comments during the party, let the pros know, and make sure to give each a list of important moments you don't want to miss.

decorations

Choose decorations that are beautiful but understated. Make an effort not to be wasteful, and remember that less is often more when it comes to pretty details.

Avoid random decor (like pedestals with giant arrangements just sitting in the middle of a room), and focus on the visual centers of each room (fire-places, entrances, and so forth).

Treat centerpieces as accents rather than over-the-top creations. I am a fan of low arrangements to promote conversation, but if your space or your wishes favor something with more scale, work with your designer to create something elegant that won't totally obstruct guests' views of the dance floor, speeches, or each other. After all, it's about sharing a moment together, right?

If possible, try to give away or reuse your flowers. If you'll have a brunch the next day, perhaps you can incorporate them. Don't inconvenience guests to move things (excuse me, Uncle Bob, I just need to grab that flower arrangement to move it over here); just be mindful that when you are fortu-nate enough to party amid an abundance of food, flowers, and good wishes, it is wise to appreciate the heck out of them.

Reception
DOS & DON'TS

DO

- Provide transportation to and from the reception for any guests who might need it. Consider your location, the hours of the party, and whether or not alcohol will be served.

- Instruct your vendors in advance about details such as the name of a contact person to whom they should speak if an issue or problem arises on the big day, along with rules and regulations at your reception venue.

- Find out if your vendors will need meals or other consideration (such as storage for equipment) during the party. These details are usually specified in your contracts with service providers, but it is always gracious to take care of those who will work so hard to make your day perfect.

DON'T

- Resist the temptation to offer a cash bar at your reception. Just because you've seen it before does not make it right. It is better to serve only beer and wine than to make your guests pay for drinks.

- Don't seat people together who may have conflict with one another. Pay special mind to sensitive feelings when it comes to seating, but do remember that as long as you are gracious in your planning, your guests are expected to go the extra mile to get along for this important occasion.

- Waste not. Try to be mindful of conserving resources wherever possible, whether it's using recycled paper for your menus, eliminating an unnecessary food station, or simply donating or reusing some of the flowers from your gorgeous party.

just MARRIED

After the reception, you'll spend your first night together as a married couple. Enjoy the moment. Take time to look into each other's eyes and share your happiness, your excitement, your passion.

If you'll stay in the same hotel as your guests, make sure to request a room situated away from the hubbub so that you'll have your privacy. Remember to put your "Don't Disturb" sign on the door!

If a friend or family member will host a post-wedding brunch in your honor the next day, you are not obligated to appear, but if you are still in town, it is a really nice opportunity to reminisce about the fabulous time you had and to say goodbye to guests who might be returning home.

hold the honeymoon

I strongly suggest waiting at least a day before leaving on your honeymoon, if for no other reason than to give you time to nap, pack, and hang up your wedding dress before you jet off. Stick the cake top in the freezer, let the best man return the rented clothes, and call a limousine to take you to the airport!

wedding announcements

There are two types of wedding announcements. The first are published by newspapers, typically in their society pages. They usually appear just before or after the wedding takes place, and for larger papers, submissions are reviewed and accepted based on varying criteria. At least three months before your wedding, check your local paper's website or call their editorial offices to find out the requirements for submitting your wedding announcement.

Newlywed

DO

- Keep writing those thank-you notes, until they're completely finished. Every last one of them. Even if you're late. Even if it's been months.

- Keep the romance of your engagement going strong as newlyweds. Leave notes for each other, arrange date nights, and do little things you know will please your new spouse.

- Invite folks over for cocktail parties or festive feasts. Start a revolving dinner party and take turns hosting it. Use all the gifts you got for the wedding—cookware, china, crystal, linens. Celebrate and enjoy!

- To help you prepare for all the get-togethers you'll host, start a party pantry. Set aside a cupboard or closet and collect fun placemats, napkin rings, vases, and other entertaining supplies so that you'll be ready in an instant with inspiration and great details if you decide to have friends over.

DON'T

- Don't send wedding announcements to anyone who received an invitation to the wedding. Announcements are only for those who were not on the guest list, such as business associates or distant relatives or friends. And don't expect a gift, as an announcement does not obligate the recipient to send one.

- Don't forget to thank vendors or other special people who helped you with the wedding. If your caterer was amazing or your florist went above and beyond, or if your niece helped by babysitting young children at the celebration, make sure to share your appreciation.

The other type of wedding announcement is a card printed by the couple or their families, typically mailed out immediately following the wedding, to share the news with those who were not included on the guest list. Although traditionally it was sent by the bride's family, these days an announcement can be sent by either or both sets of parents or by the couple themselves. Typically, an announcement will include the date and place of the wedding.

> *Mr. and Mrs. Robert Johnson*
> *have the honor to announce*
> *the marriage of their daughter*
> *Elizabeth Anne*
> *to*
> *Mr. Jeffrey Barronfeld*
> *Saturday, the eighth of May*
> *Two thousand and ten*
> *Lake Placid, New York*

what the heck is an at-home card?

An at-home card is a way of making sure everyone knows your new address as a married couple. It's also an opportunity to share the fact that you're changing (or keeping) your name. Most couples insert an at-home card into the wedding announcement envelope. Here's a sample of the wording for an at-home card.

> *Mr. and Mrs. John Simmons*
> *will be at home*
> *after June 4th*
> *825 West 187th Street*
> *Apartment 800*
> *New York, New York 10033*

If you're keeping your maiden name, just list that instead of Mr. and Mrs.

STICKY SITUATION	SIMPLE STUNNING SOLUTION
My new husband still acts as if he's single, going out with friends all the time instead of spending evenings at home.	A good marriage is founded upon good communication. Good communication is founded upon respect. Talk to your husband, but also listen to him, and suggest, with kindness, that you come up with a plan together to make sure you see enough of him while still giving him his time with friends.
We have wildly different taste in furniture. How can we decorate together?	Either embrace an eclectic style, or pick rooms in the house that you each can decorate in your preferred style. Talk it through to see what works best for you.
We registered for fine china, but I don't want to let it just sit in a closet. Do we have to save it for special occasions?	By all means, break it out and use it! Set a fabulous table for two or host weekly dinner parties with good friends. You can't take it with you, so enjoy your beautiful things now.
What do we do about money? Should we merge our bank accounts?	The question of money is a touchy subject, and for every couple the answer is unique. You should talk about what works best for you. Perhaps it's opening a joint account for large purchases and monthly expenses, but keeping separate accounts for your own spending money.
I don't want to change my name and my new husband's family is offended.	It is your prerogative to change or keep your name. Discuss the topic with your new husband first, and explain why your own name means so much to you. Also, consider printing an at-home card to let friends and family know how you'd like to be addressed.

changing your name

If you'd like to change your name after the wedding, wait until after the honeymoon to do so, as you don't want to encounter problems with your travel reservations and your identification documents not matching.

For more information on changing your name, consult your local government office or website or search "wedding" and "name change" on the Internet for a range of packages that will help you through the process depending upon your state.

marrying your styles

If this is the first time you'll live together, you may find yourselves adjusting to each other on many levels. Personal preferences, taste in furniture, daily habits—these might all be new to you as individuals and as a couple. Always be considerate, even when you are frustrated or confused, and speak to each other with respect and admiration, even if you are dealing with a difficult situation.

If you've lived together for some time, you'll no doubt experience a change in perspective as it relates to your home life and your daily routine together. Avoid pointing out that things need to change "now that we're married," and apply a beginner's mind to any difficult situations. After all, you are beginners at being married. You are newlyweds even if you've been together for a long while.

Approaching your newly merged lives from the perspective of creating unity and with the goal of always working together in harmony as a team, you'll find you're stronger together than you ever imagined.

being a great host and a great guest

If you like to entertain, continue the festive spirit of your wedding with get-togethers on a regular basis. Invite various groups of interesting people and try your hand at introducing folks you think will find each other fascinating.

wit and wisdom

for the host

Manners are a sensitive awareness of the feelings of others. If you have that awareness, you have good manners, no matter what fork you use.

—EMILY POST

A centerpiece for the table should never be anything prepared by a taxidermist.

—ANONYMOUS

Good manners have much to do with the emotions. To make them ring true, one must feel them, not merely exhibit them.

—AMY VANDERBILT

Serve the dinner backward, do anything—but for goodness sake, do something weird.

—ELSA MAXWELL

Those who have mastered etiquette, who are entirely, impeccably right, would seem to arrive at a point of exquisite dullness.

—DOROTHY PARKER

A host is like a general: calamities often reveal his genius.

—HORACE

Respect for ourselves guides our morals. Respect for others guides our manners.

—LAURENCE STERNE

At a dinner party one should eat wisely but not too well, and talk well but not too wisely.

—WILLIAM SOMERSET MAUGHAM

If it's against state law, it's generally considered a breach of etiquette.

—JUDITH MARTIN ("Miss Manners")

on communication

The first duty of love is to listen.

—PAUL TILLICH

When angry, count ten before you speak; if very angry, a hundred.

—THOMAS JEFFERSON

Kind words do not cost much. Yet they accomplish much.

—BLAISE PASCAL

when emotions run high and stress threatens to get the best of us

There is no use worrying about things over which you have no control, and if you have control, you can do something about them instead of worrying.

—STANLEY C. ALLYN

Patience and perseverance have a magical effect before which difficulties disappear and obstacles vanish.

—JOHN QUINCY ADAMS

I think the next best thing to solving a problem is finding some humor in it.

—FRANK A. CLARK

on love and marriage

There is no more lovely, friendly, and charming relationship, communion, or company than a good marriage.

—MARTIN LUTHER

Neither a lofty degree of intelligence nor imagination nor both together go to the making of genius. Love, love, love, that is the soul of genius.

—WOLFGANG AMADEUS MOZART

This is the miracle that happens every time to those who really love; the more they give, the more they possess.

—RAINER MARIA RILKE

To keep your marriage brimming, With love in the loving cup, Whenever you're wrong admit it; Whenever you're right shut up.

—OGDEN NASH

resource guide

If you're looking for in-depth help or inspiration on a particular subject, check out the other books in my Simple Stunning series, including the Simple Stunning Wedding Organizer, a workbook and binder that walks you through all the steps of planning your perfect celebration. Also, check out my website and blog at www.karenbussen.com. These are some of my favorite resources, organized by chapter.

rules of engagement

BOOKS

Wedding Rings by Osnat Gad offers a beautiful look at the subject.

With This Ring: The Ultimate Guide to Wedding Jewelry by Penny Proddow and Marion Fasel

ONLINE

www.bluenile.com sells a variety of rings and is a great place for research.
www.weddingwindow.com gets you started with your own wedding website.

OTHER

Check your local newspaper for guidelines on publishing engagement announcements.

money matters

BOOKS

1001 Ways to Save Money . . . and Still Have a Dazzling Wedding by Sharon Naylor

Bridal Bargains: Secrets to Throwing a Fantastic Wedding on a Realistic Budget by Denise Fields. This book offers links and information for lots of money-saving ideas and resources.

ONLINE

www.theknot.com and www.brides.com both have good budget tools.

SOFTWARE

Programs such as Excel offer the opportunity to create a personal spreadsheet for budgets and payments.

bridal party basics

ONLINE

www.ourweddingday.com is full of great guest list tools, including an address book that allows you to email guests requesting their addresses. Their reply prompts an automatic update to your address book.

www.brides.com is the best place for bridal clothing. It includes links to thousands of photos grouped by designer, plus articles about styles, accessories, and other fashion information. You can also find information and links to men's bridal attire here.

www.threaddesign.com is a bridesmaid (and flower girl) dress design company with a great website and lots of styles in different fabrics like organza, chiffon, and satin.

invitation only

BOOKS

Wedding Invitations by Jennifer Cegielski

ONLINE AND RETAIL

INVITATIONS

www.cecinewyork.com offers couture invitations and stationery.
www.dauphinepress.com
www.mygatsby.com

www.weddingpaperdivas.com
www.indianweddingcard.com

DIGITAL CALLIGRAPHY

www.inkspun.com

PAPER

www.katespaperie.com
www.mountaincow.com
www.paperpresentation.com
www.paper-source.com
www.printicon.com

POSTAGE

www.photo.stamps.com lets you add a photo to your postage.
www.cecinewyork.com offers custom stamps.
www.usps.com has every stamp that's currently available for sale.

SOFTWARE

Printing Press Wedding Software for Invitations
The Complete Social Publisher
AllType Professional Calligraphy, Handwriting, and Script Fonts Collection is calligraphy software for printing envelopes.

please and thank you

BOOKS

The Ultimate Wedding Registry Workbook: Choosing the Best Wedding Gifts for Your Life Together by Sharon Naylor

ONLINE

www.myregistry.com lets you create your own custom registry from multiple online retailers.

www.themanregistry.com is an Amazon store featuring a collection of items for the bride and groom.

www.amazon.com also offers general wedding registry for your favorite cookbooks, a set of the classics, wonderful novels in hardcover, or art/coffee table tomes in addition to a lot of other good stuff.

www.maxwellsilver.com has an enormous selection of flatware.

www.mossonline.com offers chic home accessories by a range of contemporary designers.

www.conranusa.com
www.morrellwine.com is great for creating a fine wine registry.

www.sherry-lehman.com is another great wine resource.

www.idofoundation.org lets you create a charity registry or link your gift registry to a charity, so that part of the proceeds from gifts purchased benefit a good cause.

satellite celebrations

BOOKS

My book *Simple Stunning Wedding Showers* has ideas, recipes, and games for twenty fabulous shower themes.

The Everything Bachelorette Party: Throw a Party That the Bride and Her Friends Will Never Forget by Jennifer Rung and Shelly Hagen

ONLINE

www.adventurebachelorparty.com organizes great trips for the outdoorsy groom.

the ceremony

BOOKS

Wedding Words: Vows by Jennifer Cegielski

I Do: A Guide to Creating Your Own Unique Wedding Ceremony by Sydney Barbara Metrick

Your Special Wedding Vows by Sharon Naylor

Vows: The African-American Couples' Guide to Designing a Sacred Ceremony by Harriette Cole

Joining Hands and Hearts: Interfaith, Intercultural Wedding Celebrations—A Practical Guide for Couples by Susanna Stefanachi Macomb and Andrea Thompson is a wonderful, thoughtful guide to creating a ceremony that embraces and honors both your traditions.

The Knot Guide to Wedding Vows and Traditions: Readings, Rituals,

Music, Dances, and Toasts by Carley Roney. This book has a lot of great information on different traditions and rituals, plus music and readings.

ONLINE

www.myweddingvows.com offers inspiration, poems, traditional, and multi-cultural vows.
www.worldweddingtraditions.com This easy-to-use website offers simple descriptions and inspirations for wedding ceremonies and celebrations throughout the world and across all cultures.

party perfect

BOOKS

Simple Stunning Weddings: Designing and Creating Your Perfect Celebration is my design book filled with almost 200 photos of ideas and inspirations for every kind of wedding.

My book *Simple Stunning Wedding Flowers* offers inspiration for bouquets, centerpieces, and floral accents, as well as helpful flower reference charts.

Wedding Words: Toasts by Jennifer Cegielski is a great resource for those who will speak at your wedding.

just married

BOOKS

The Nest Newlywed Handbook: An Owner's Manual for Modern Married Life by Carley Roney

For Richer Not Poorer: The Newlywed's Financial Survival Guide by Deborah Wilburn

Smart Couples Finish Rich: 9 Steps to Creating a Rich Future for You and Your Partner by David Bach has helped millions of people get their finances in order and understand the miracle of compound interest.

ONLINE

www.shutterfly.com allows you to create a wedding announcement card or fun gifts using your photos.
www.cecinewyork.com can design custom stationery for after the wedding.
www.thenamechangekit.com is a great site offering complete name change information and forms for every state.
www.lusciousverde.com has casual, whimsical styles and pretty papers to choose from, and offers online personalization for your note cards.
www.smythson.com The famed luxury stationer offers online ordering for personalized engraved stationery.

acknowledgments

Many thanks to the many people who have contributed their wisdom, guidance, energy, and talent to the creation of this book.

I am blessed to work with such super folks. I simply cannot help but be excited to attack every day and each project with a big smile. To my studio staff: a huge thank-you, especially to Melissa Ford, Edgar Lopez, and Eliza Coleman.

My literary agent, Joy Tutela, is a constant source of support and inspiration. My editor, Jennifer Levesque, with her enthusiastic, efficient example, motivates all those who have the pleasure of working with her. Beth Huseman, our copy editor, makes the incredibly tough job of fixing my mistakes look as easy as pie.

What can be said about Susi Oberhelman, the designer of the whole Simple Stunning series of books? She's a genius, and that's just a fact. But don't tell anybody, because I don't want her to get too busy for us.

I can never thank Leslie Stoker, my publisher, enough for her belief in the Simple Stunning message. When I'm struggling with a concept or decision, I often think of Leslie's serene presence, her elegant style, and her commitment to creating and celebrating quality.

Thanks to Josh Levenbrown at Paradigm for his smarts, his positive energy, and his eternal good advice. And, of course, mad props to my lawyer, Dan Marotta, for keeping a creative type like me on track!

Special thanks to Lisa Hoffman at Ceci New York for her gorgeous stationery designs, and to Dr. Katherine Kurs for her help and guidance with the ceremony chapter.

I come from a small family. Through my fortunate, festive collaborations with many couples and their families, I have had an opportunity to be included in so many wonderful celebrations and beautiful moments. I am truly grateful to each and every one of you, and I thank you all with a full heart.

index

This book is dedicated to the memory of my father,
Thomas Bussen, and to his lovely wife, Brenda.

Published in 2007 by
Stewart, Tabori & Chang
An imprint of Harry N. Abrams, Inc.

Photo credits: Pages 2, 20, and 100: Scott Whittle; pages 6, 12, 17, 30, 41, 78, 80 (left),
84, 104, and 112: Belathée Photography; pages 9, 50, 72, and 80 (right): Barnaby Draper Studios;
page 95: Christian Oth Photography.

Pages 9, 50, 72, 89, and 95: Stationery design by CECI New York

Library of Congress Cataloging-in-Publication Data

Bussen, Karen.
    Simple stunning wedding etiquette / Karen Bussen.
        p. cm.
    ISBN-13: 978-1-58479-649-7
    ISBN-10: 1-58479-649-9
    1. Wedding etiquette. I. Title.

BJ2051.B87 2007
395.2'2--dc22   2007012055

Editor: Jennifer Levesque
Designer: Susi Oberhelman
Production Manager: Jacquie Poirier

The text of this book was composed in Helvetica Neue and New Caledonia

Printed and bound in China

10 9 8 7 6 5 4 3 2 1

HNA
harry n. abrams, inc.
a subsidiary of La Martinière Groupe

115 West 18th Street | New York, NY 10011
www.hnabooks.com